General Thinker

Remo Giuffré

"There's a time for work, and there's a time for love.
That leaves no other time."

Coco Chanel

EOLO

General Thinker

by Remo Giuffré

Published in Australia in 2014 by
EOLO Pty Limited | ABN 33 403 341 098
PO Box 7488 Bondi Beach
Sydney NSW 2026 AUSTRALIA
Email: eolo@generalthinking.com

Printed in China

Remo would like to acknowledge and thank:

Adam Dennis, Melanie Giuffré, Aivi Juske and Eileen Gittins, along with:

Jaki Arthur, Dominique Antarakis, Chris Anderson and all at TED, Julia Beavan, Cheryl Bart, Fleur Brown and all at Launch Group, all my friends at the Bondi Icebergs (including my morning sauna buddies), Sunny Bates, Peter Barrow, Peter Cramer, Amy Denmeade, Kirsty de Garis, Jill Dupleix, Joe and Jessica Dames, Yvonne Frindle, Bob Fox, Giulia Giuffré, Lola Giuffré, Roman Giuffré, Marie Giuffré (Mum), Bruno Giuffré, Sonia Giuffré, Geoffrey Gifford, Cesare Giuffré, General Thinkers all over the world, David Glover, Seth Godin, Peter Holmes à Court, Melanie Horkan, Annette Higgins, Patrick Jury and the team at Donovan Jury Law, Dare Jennings, Dennis Jones, Jon Jureidini, Maira Kalman, Michael B. Keegan, all of my Kickstarter backers, Nathan Leong, Tim Lumsdaine, Nigel Marsh, Fran Moore, Julian Morrow, Ann Mossop and all at Sydney Opera House, Nanette Moulton, Damien O'Brien, Theo Pettaras, Diana Prichard and all the crew from Dinner at Mum's, Mark E Pollack, all REMO General Store alumni wherever you are in the world, Douglas Riccardi, everyone who's ever lost any money investing in a version of REMO, Andrew Rothery, REMO Customers, Tom Rielly, Kevin Roberts, Anton Rosenberg and all at Claymore Capital, Janne Ryan, Stefan Sagmeister, Mark Scott and all at ABC, Sid Soin and all at Countplus, Erik Spiekermann, Mark Stott, Lara Stein, the TEDxSydney team (past and present), Maurice Terzini and all at Icebergs Dining Room and Bar, my many TEDster friends, Tucker Viemeister and Richard Saul Wurman

ORDERING GENERAL THINKER

General Thinker is available online at **blurb.com/generalthinker** or via **amazon.com**. An EPUB version for the iPad is also available via Blurb or the Apple iBooks Store.

Quantity discounts are auto applied at **blurb.com/generalthinker**.

Please direct all **trade** sale enquiries via email to **remo@generalthinking.com**.

remogiuffre.com/generalthinker

The National Library of Australia
Cataloguing-in-Publication Data

Author: Giuffré, Remo
Title: General Thinker | Remo Giuffré

ISBN: 978-0-9925848-0-1 (paperback: stitched), 978-0-9925848-2-5 (paperback: pod), 978-0-9925848-1-8 (ebook: epub), 978-0-9925848-3-2 (ebook: pdf)

Includes Index

Subjects: 1. Giuffré, Remo 2. Giuffré, Remo – Philosophy 3. REMO (Firm : Sydney, New South Wales) – History 4. Businesspeople – New South Wales – Biography 5. Stores, Retail – New South Wales – History 6. Entrepreneurship – Anecdotes 7. Marketing – Anecdotes 8. Design – Anecdotes

Dewey Number: 338.092

General Thinker

Remo Giuffré

for

Melanie, Lola & Roman

EOLO

Table of Contents

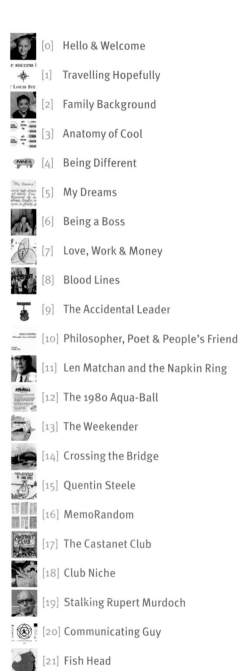
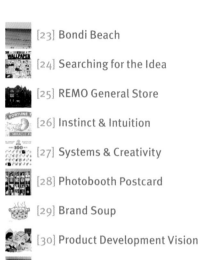

[87]

[88]

[o] Hello & Welcome

Welcome to General Thinker.

As a serial founder, entrepreneur and brand builder I have experienced both great success and brilliant failure in my life to date, all the while learning lots about myself and others. This book tells the stories and examines the experiences that have guided and shaped me along the path.

It's a book about work. It's a book about love. (What else is there? Thanks Coco.)

It's a personal memoir, but also about people, experiences and brands, and an ongoing exploration of what it takes to engage, delight and create desire.

The people who were close to me during the heyday of the REMO General Store [Chapter 25] all sensed that we were playing a role in something epic, and it would often be said to me in the wake of something good or bad that had happened: *"That'll be a chapter for the book."*

So, I guess that "the book" was always something that was going to happen one day.

Also, there have been other episodes in my life that I felt would be good stories in the telling e.g. my courtship of Melanie [38] or my "travelling hopefully" epiphany [1].

This book of visual memoirs tells those stories in a way that best suits my skills and preferences as a design communicator and merchant; and like a merchandise catalogue, it can be read chronologically, or randomly and in chunks. Whatever suits.

Finally, this is not the first time that I've tried to get this book written and published. Every five or so years for the past 10 or 15 I have had a crack at it, deciding on each occasion that it wasn't the right time. Then this year it all came together, thanks in part to a chance connection with Blurb Founder and CEO Eileen Gittins at the 2014 TED Conference [45]. A simpatico Eileen felt that the time for General Thinker was nigh, and offered to help make it all happen. She gave me just over a month to write and design it, and I duly complied. It's amazing how quickly things flow when the timing is finally right.

I think you'll find this book interesting. I hope that it also inspires you in some way.

Remo Giuffré
General Thinker | Bondi Beach [23]

[1] Travelling Hopefully

I remember feeling optimistic.

It was late July 2001 in the middle of the North American summer. I was sitting with my wife Melanie and my kids Lola and Roman on the ferry that connects the town of Bayshore with the beachside communities of Fire Island just east of New York. We were heading to a tiny but special place called Lonelyville [59]. Until recently we had owned a house within this idyllic beachside community; the first piece of real property that Melanie and I had ever managed to own together. But soon after buying it, and for various reasons, we decided to shift our lives and the young family back to Sydney; so we needed to sell the house in Lonelyville in order to fund the move back home.

We'd been living in the US for almost four years, mostly in New York City, but prior to that in Silicon Valley. I had been working as a consultant Brand Strategist, a gun for hire "guru," working mostly with Internet-related businesses. That was my day job. In parallel to this, I had been endeavouring to relaunch the REMO General Store online [54]. Despite a unique vision, my ongoing efforts to revive the venture, and a large number of high-powered advisors and supporters, REMO was still in the hibernation it had entered upon its untimely demise (for financial and administrative reasons) back in 1996 [49]. For more years than I care to recall I had been pitching venture capitalists, corporations and wealthy individual investors with my vision for a next generation webcentric REMO General Store, smart and profitable ... but to no avail. The business was too quirky, the timing was never good. The rejections were countless [82]. However, a meeting taken in California with Maheesh Jain and Fred Durham, the founders of a print-on-demand T shirt business called Cafepress.com, just a few days before, had gently fanned my eternal REMO flame by revealing a way that might enable us to get a REMO T shirts website transactional for a very modest (and Melanie-approved) capital outlay.

So I felt optimistic.

Not only do I remember feeling optimistic, but I also remember coming to the realisation that this feeling of optimism was probably more important than whatever was going to happen. A feeling of optimism about the future, thankfully shared by Melanie, was delivering us a very high quality of life in the present. The outcomes of our endeavours were actually irrelevant to the quality of the lives we were living!

A few days later I spoke of this personal epiphany over the phone with a great friend and supporter in LA who rewarded me with this sage quote from Robert Louis Stevenson:

"To travel hopefully is a better thing than to arrive, and the true success is to labour."

Ever since, I've tried to live life with this liberating truth very much in mind.

To travel hopefully
is a better thing than to arrive,
and the true success is to labour.

ROBERT LOUIS STEVENSON
1850~1894

[80]

Lonelyville, FI   On the ferry to FI   Lonelyville house   Lola, Roman and Wagon   REMO T shirt

1 2 3 4 5 6 7 8 9 10 11 12 13 14 15 16 17 18 19 20 21 22 23 24 25 26 27 28 29 30 31 32 33 34 35 36 37 38 39 40 41 42 43 44 45 46 47 48 49 50 51 52 53 54

2001

[2] Family Background

No real life lessons on this page. Just a bit of background to set the scene.

I was a cute baby and child. *C'mon, admit it.* Born in 1960 and named Remo after Remus as in Romulus and Remus, the she-wolf-sucking twin founders of Rome. I was apparently also named after a charming Lothario-type my parents had met while on a Flotta Lauro cruise.

My suburban Sydney Italo-Australian childhood was a happy and stable one. Both parents of Italian heritage. Mum (née de Lorenzo) born in Redfern, but Dad born on a tiny Æolian island off the coast of Sicily, migrating here on his own as a 15 year old in 1928. He made good as a self-taught designer and businessman. He did very well for himself and our family, initially as a florist with a small chain of shops in Sydney's Eastern Suburbs, and then as a manufacturer of various things (cosmetic packaging, costume jewellery, aluminium furniture, etc.) Dad was also very engaged in service to the community: as a Rotarian, as a pillar of the Italian immigrant community (he was the founder of a government funded agency called *Co.As.It*, and was formally honoured by the Italian government first as a *Commendatore* and ultimately as a *Grande Ufficiale*), and, possibly most importantly, as the go-to guy and padrone for newly arrived Italians who needed a leg up. I lost count of the people and businesses that he funded, and indeed one of his factories in Camperdown, *Popolare*, was referred to as the "iron lung" in reference to the fact that, in the day, just about every Italian immigrant arriving in Sydney survived thanks to their first job there. Somewhere to start in the new country.

There were four of us kids, and we were (and are still) all so similar yet different: **Giulia**, the Oxford-educated whip-smart PhD academic; **Bruno**, the diligent genius radiologist (every extended Italian family needs its doctor); **Sonia**, the theatrically trained and quintessentially crafty design services producer; and me, the black sheep entrepreneur, who always seemed to be working so hard, but who also always appeared to be on the verge of going broke.

I was a wilful, discontented little boy. My Nonna on Mum's side (a super colourful Neapolitan who managed the dividends of her sons Vincent and Tony de Lorenzo's stellar hairdressing business [8]) used to send prayers to Pompeii for the redemption of my soul. Having said that, she was also an early and intuitive believer in me and used to tell Mum her sense was that I would do something special with my life. However, I think she was imagining something more along the lines of a violin-playing virtuoso than a gifted merchant.

Later on, at school, I tended to be a bit on the anxious side, and the only thing that served to calm me down were big doses of extra curricular mathematics, specifically problem solving. It went like this ...

Problems Posed › Problems Solved › Answers Offered › Answers Checked at Back of Book › Answers CORRECT =› Anxious Remo Soothed

So, that's the background. I'm sure you get the picture.

Remo, Giulia, Sonia and Bruno

Baby Remo

The Capitoline Wolf

Dad the Rotarian

Mum and Dad

Nonna

Popolare factory

Being a Boss [8]

1 2 3 4 5 6 7 8 9 10 11 12 13 14 15 16 17 18 19 20 21 22 23 24 25 26 27 28 29 30 31 32 33 34 35 36 37 38 39 40 41 42 43 44 45 46 47 48 49 50 51 52 53 54

1960   1966

[3] Anatomy of Cool

What's cool? What's daggy? Who decides?

Dictionary definitions of the word "cool" containing words like "excellent" or "first rate" are very unsatisfying and, by definition, totally *uncool*. Anyway, *you* know what I mean by "cool," just as most Australians know what is meant by the opposite word "daggy." To a certain extent, both words are really better defined by their application and usage.

I learned something about the anatomy (and alchemy) of cool by observing how a guy named Bob D'Angelo kept his school pants up in Sydney's Eastern Suburbs circa 1973.

Bob D'Angelo, a new boy from the US, was a very cool guy. You could feel it in your bones. Strong and silent. Nice physique. Straight long blonde hair. Good surfer.

But then there was Bob D'Angelo's belt. It was black, woven and elasticised with an heraldic metal clasp at the front and adjustable sliders at the hips. That belt was regarded at the time as the epitome of dagginess and very uncool … *until* Bob wore the belt to school, and then it became cool. Voila!

This demonstration of alchemy and other experiences over time have led me to believe:

1. Some people are naturally cool or not cool;
2. Some things are inherently cool or not cool;
3. Cool people can make things cool, but cool things can't make people cool.

PS: Is it possible, do you think, that someone could eventually make Splayds [35] cool?

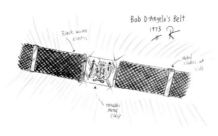

Bob D'Angelo's belt, 1973

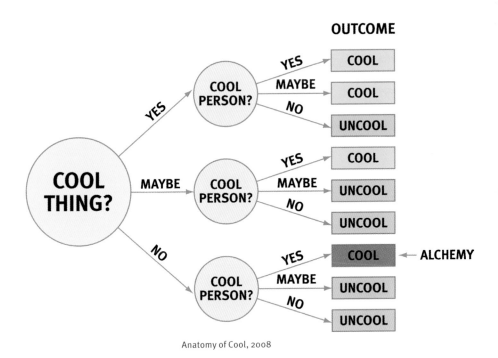

OUTCOME

Anatomy of Cool, 2008

FORM 2B
Back Row: S. Maniaci, J. Keona, P. Brown, G. Peters, C. Turner, A. Lumsden.
Third Row: P. O'Kane, A. Varnava, M. Ryan, B. Walsh, A. Shaw, R. Gioffre, V. Nave.
Second Row: A. Miles, R. D'Angelo, J. Sciberras, P. Russell, D. Harrigan, J. Quigley, A. Reynolds, A. Scipione.
Front Row: G. Moloney, R. Foord, B. Byrnes, A. Kava, B. McCabe, M. Rouesnel, M. Ellis, G. Peek.
Absent: T. Forsyth.

Form 2B, Waverley College, 1973

[4] Being Different

We lived in Kensington and I attended a couple of Catholic schools in Randwick and then Waverley College for the rest of my schooling.

As an Australian of Italian parentage, I was already near the outside edge of what was, in those days, a mainstream Anglo-Saxon society. Some kids in my neighbourhood were at pains to make that distinction. I remember having my "Surfa Sam" skateboard stolen at the local handball court in Kensington. It stayed missing for weeks. Our parish priest was eventually able to extract it from the local hoods. Even so, they decided that they should help me not lose it again by blow torching the word "WOG" across the deck. Nice.

During those younger school years I was something of a maths geek (nicknamed "the professor" by the Brigidine sisters) and a high achiever (dux of the class every year like my brother and sister before me).

At the Christian Brothers-run Waverley College the dominant tribes were: rugby jocks, surfies and the boarders. I didn't really fit into any of these camps, but I was actually associating with most of them [9] ... albeit typically in a somewhat peripheral role e.g. a footy player, but not a very good one; or hanging out with the girls on Maroubra Beach while the proper surfers (with real physical courage) rode the waves.

Finally, in terms of family influence, the expectation placed on all of us kids was that we would all somehow excel: *"If you can't come first, at least come in the top three."*

The combination of these strengths and shortcomings did make me feel a bit different, and the part of me that wanted to belong as an Aussie wasn't always happy about that.

Anyway, at some point in my late teens (I can't recall exactly when) being a bit different stopped being something I was embarrassed about ... and started being something I was happy to celebrate. That was a turning point. I was now much more curious about my Italian heritage (although regrettably unable to speak the language) and I became so attracted to my own identity that for some years I wore my actual gold *"Remo"* baby pin on my adult lapel.

These days I am a diehard multiculturalist #, and I enjoy living in a much more racially diverse Australia where just about everyone you meet is, by definition, different.

As a leader of the Italian community in Australia, my father was a foundation member of the Multicultural Committee initiated by the Australian Government and chaired by Frank Galbally.

Remo in the front row holding the footy

| Bum shuffler Remo never crawled | That hat is *not* right | Surfing trip with Bob and Ray, 1973 | Wearing the baby pin | REMO Baby Pins for sale in catalogue |

[5] My Dreams

The ability of champion athletes to be able to imagine their subsequent victories with some lucidity is well documented. (That's French for: *"Take my word for it, as I'm not going to be citing any research here."*)

Imagining victory is a life skill that most of us are born with, but which the majority of us lose. It's an age thing. Virtually every child imagines him or herself scoring the winning try/goal or hitting the winning run. But the stats are not great. Usually only one person gets the opportunity to be that hero. It's human nature for us to imagine *ourselves* to be that person, *until* those dreams get knocked out of us by the harsh realities of ability and circumstance.

Not too many adults retain that desire to be the winning hero. We are too busy imagining failure, which is a pity. However, for some of us, failure is simply to be regarded as delayed success. It's a better way to travel. More hope. Less angst. See Chapter [1].

And in this respect, *My Dreams* are a case in point:

Individual sporting prowess was not really my thing at school, although I did enjoy myself on the footy field and, paradoxically, was generally a member of the winning team.

This bit of writing by my 13-year-old self (for which Brother Hay gave me an A) is somewhat telling … full of enthusiasm and hope, but just a little bit sad there toward the end. Or maybe not.

It seems that our characters and thought patterns are set when we are quite young.

Early and consistent underachievement in the school sporting arena was a reinforcement of the fact that, for me, participation and an enduring sense of HOPE were more important than any ultimate result.

1968

"My Dreams"

R. Giuffre
1 b

I can't help dreaming. It's a sort of habit. I'm always looking forward to something like Christmas, Easter, my birthday or even a footy game. I dream about anything worth waiting for.

Take for instance a footy game. I often spend my Friday nights running up and down the hall with a pillow, practising my tackles. I'm alway scoring tries at home but never on the field.

When I look forward to something I really get involved. I dream about it

Composition, 1973

1 2 3 4 5 6 7 8 9 10 11 12 13 14 15 16 17 18 19 20 21 22 23 24 25 26 27 28 29 30 31 32 33 34 35 36 37 38 39 40 41 42 43 44 45 46 47 48 49 50 51 52 53 54

1973

[6] Being a Boss

My father ran a number of businesses over the course of a very successful and entrepreneurial migrant-done-good career. During my teens his focus was a company called Kentcast (tagline: *Elegance in Aluminium*) that was in the business of designing, manufacturing and selling a range of cast aluminium furniture. (Australians would know the stuff. It was the ubiquitous white patio furniture of the 70s.) The factory was in Sydney's Marrickville and it employed hundreds of people hailing originally from dozens of different countries. It was a multicultural melting pot.

Dad's role was to take the risks … and then to envision, design and lead. The design process often happened at our kitchen table in Kensington, and usually on a napkin. I witnessed the birth of many tables and chairs … and the occasional example of design ingenuity, for instance the big-selling magazine stand started life as two chair backs connected at the base.

Every Christmas holidays I would spend weeks working at "the factory." Because I was the "boss's son" and because this is how it works in life, I would be given the most challenging jobs and ridden hard by Hank Meekels, the Dutch foreman. I recall one brain cell-destroying week where I did nothing other than dunk raw aluminium chairs into a vat of acetone.

Dad was a hands-on leader, the kind of guy who knows everyone's name and family situation. He would walk the factory floor naturally and with genuine interest. No silk suit or Italian leather shoe was so shiny that it couldn't be scuffed by the oily black sand they used to cast the aluminium components in the foundry. Back in the office, it was all cigarette smoke and deals sealed with a handshake. Oscar Schindler meets Don Corleone.

In summary, during a formative period of my life, I was able to spend a lot of time observing an empathetic and engaged leadership style that generated only love and respect.

So it's obvious, in retrospect, that Dad was my most influential leadership role model.

In February 1986, while I was still living in New York, I received word that Dad's health was failing and that he probably only had days left to live. Two days before he died, I included these words to him in a farewell letter written from New York:

"As a father you are an ideal role model for your children: – strong yet compassionate. All of us kids owe both you and Mum a tremendous amount. You gave us many gifts which we use daily. You gave us the courage to be different and the motivation to dare to do things in new ways. You gave us all leadership: – the burning desire to lead and not follow, to stand up and be counted. You also gave us a sense of what was right and what was wrong. Most importantly, you gave us strength. From you and from Mum we inherit a tremendous internal strength. This strength tells us that if we set out to achieve something, then we <u>can achieve it</u>. It enables us to carry through our plans with confidence. It tells us not to be satisfied unless we commit ourselves 100%. For this strength – we thank you."

[76]

Dad in his office at Popolare in Camperdown

Commendatore Giuffré

Kentcast leadership

elegance in aluminium

Magazine rack

Letter to Dad
February 1986

OBITUARY
Leader in Italian community

Mr Gaetano Annibale (Tom) Giuffre, one of the founding fathers of Italian self-help community welfare in Sydney, has died aged 74.

Mr Giuffre arrived in Sydney in 1928 aged 15 and founded the Italian Welfare Centre in 1950. He was the founder and first president of Co.As.It (Comitato Assistenziale Italiano) in 1968.

Co.As.It. is one of the principal providers of welfare assistance to the Italian community and has taken a lead in promoting Italian culture and language in the wider Australian community.

From small beginnings with a florist's shop in Paddington, Mr Giuffre went on to a successful business career.

Although a naturalised Australian, Mr Giuffre was interned briefly during World War II.

He was honoured by both the Australian and Italian governments.

The Sydney Morning Herald obituary, February 1986

1 2 3 4 5 6 7 8 9 10 11 12 13 **14** 15 16 17 18 19 20 21 22 23 24 25 26 27 **28** 29 30 31 32 33 34 35 36 37 38 39 40 41 42 43 44 45 46 47 48 49 50 51 52 53 54

1974   1986

[7] Love, Work & Money

This doodled RemoGram from 2002 is a long-time favourite.

There's what you LOVE to do. There's what you're objectively GOOD at. And finally, there's what will enable you to earn enough MONEY to live.

If you're not already in the place of equilibrium where the three circles intersect, then you should be heading there with all due haste … but from the direction as indicated.

Start with **passion**.

Life is too short to waste time doing work that doesn't bring JOY … to yourself and others.

PS: I've included a *bonus* RemoGram on this spread for good measure. This matrix dates back to 2004 when I was trying to make sense of career choices that continually pushed me into the top right quadrant where autonomy is high and content very specific.

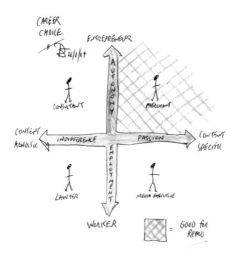

Validating my career path in 2004

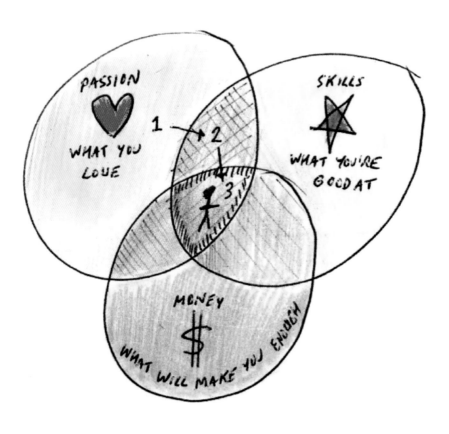

1 2 3 4 5 6 7 8 9 10 11 12 13 14 15 16 17 18 19 20 21 22 23 24 25 26 27 28 29 30 31 32 33 34 35 36 37 38 39 40 41 42 43 44 45 46 47 48 49 50 51 52 53 54

2002

[8] Blood Lines

There are a lot of entrepreneurs in my family, and that has surely had much to do with what I have chosen to do with *my* work life, to the extent that I had any choice [86].

My father was the most obvious influence. He was a lifelong entrepreneur [2].

And it was only after I opened my own store [25] in Sydney that I discovered that my paternal grandfather Vincenzo had run the local store on the Æolian island of Salina.

Possibly an even higher profile example of entrepreneurialism is provided by my uncles on Mum's side, Vincent and Tony de Lorenzo. The "boys" started out as barbers and went on to develop a thriving de Lorenzo hairdressing business on Castlereagh Street in Sydney. "Mr Anton" and "Mr Vincent." Fancy and continental. For a while there in the 60s it was *the* place for women to get their hair done in Sydney. Then, in the 70s, they took that retail profile and developed a full range of "Delva" (**de L**, **V**incent, **A**nthony) hair products, distributed widely, but exclusively via hairdressing salons. Vin also fronted a weekly five-minute television demonstration programme called "Hair Care with de Lorenzo", complete with comically blue-rinsed models. That gave the brand a significant national profile, and Delva was ultimately sold for a handsome price to Reckitt & Coleman, a multinational corporation.

My uncles and father formed a good team and business was good. Tony was the meticulous chemist. Vin was the creative marketer. Dad was the sage impartial Chairman. Vin was also my Godfather, although we weren't particularly close. Even so, I do recall in positive terms the enthusiasm with which he would show off the latest Delva product development. He seemed to be having fun. I noticed that.

My Uncle Luigi (married to my father's younger sister, Lisetta) also ran his own business, the Ravioli & Lasagna Kitchen in Sydney's Neutral Bay. As an aside, that business was my first external "client." I wrote the copy and designed their brand identity while I was still at law school. They retained that hand-drawn logo for a long time.

Finally, closer to home, and more relevantly for our kids in terms of *their* influences, my wife Melanie has never really worked for anyone other than herself. She started her own photographic agency in Paris in her early 20s and moved it to Australia in the late 80s. Melanie Dames Agency, operating during the prime years of the REMO General Store, was highly regarded and actually a much more profitable business than REMO ever was.

Nature or nurture? The debate is moot. Certainly, I copped it from both barrels.

THE BEGGAR BOY HAIRCUT
Modelled by... GIULIA ANNA GIUFFRE

Residents of Salina in 1932. Nonno Vincenzo Giuffré front row with crossed arms holding hat.

Dad

Tony and Vin

Nonna with
de Lorenzo press

"This is Your Life"
Vincent de Lorenzo

My logo design for Uncle Luigi

Cleo magazine, 1990

Courting Melanie Dames [38]

1 2 3 4 5 6 7 8 9 10 11 12 13 14 15 16 17 18 19 20 21 22 23 24 25 26 27 28 29 30 31 32 33 34 35 36 37 38 39 40 41 42 43 44 45 46 47 48 49 50 51 52 53 54

1960   1974   1979   1991

[9] The Accidental Leader

I come from a long line of School Captains ... everyone in the family actually, except my father, who didn't finish his schooling, so that doesn't count.

My mother and both of my sisters were School Captains at Brigidine Convent in Randwick, and my brother Bruno had been the School Captain at Waverley College six years before I was eligible for the post.

Even so, it's not something that I necessarily aspired to for myself. After all, I wasn't really like my siblings. I was the black sheep who had little regard for formal authority. Being a school prefect didn't really fit with my brand positioning as a maverick teen.

But the other thing I had was a short attention span and a low boredom threshold. So what I would do during the lunch hour at school is very naturally shift from group to group and tribe to tribe: a bit of handball with the jocks, some time with the wogs, a few jokes with the boarders, a distracted moment or two with the surfies, finishing up with a bit of good natured ribbing of the nerds.

This behaviour made me very popular purely by virtue of the fact I was quite literally the only person that everybody knew. And so, when it came time for everyone to come together to vote for the Year 12 prefects, I became the default selection for all sorts of people ... and won by a landslide: The Accidental Leader.

My elevation and coronation as head boy of the Big School was a bit unexpected and raised a few eyebrows at home. Reverence and a sense of duty were never my strong suits. But this was a case where my natural curiosity and empathy, along with my ongoing quest to be *interested*, had indirectly turned me into a popular leader.

Remo the 1977 School Captain with Dad and Mum

Mum	Giulia	Bruno	Remo	Sonia
School Captain	School Captain	School Captain	School Captain	School Captain
1945	1969	1971	1977	1979

1 2 3 4 5 6 7 8 9 10 11 12 13 14 15 16 **17** 18 19 20 21 22 23 24 25 26 27 28 29 30 31 32 33 34 35 36 37 38 39 40 41 42 43 44 45 46 47 48 49 50 51 52 53 54

1977

[10] Philosopher, Poet & People's Friend

Pretentious? *Moi?*

This was the business card that my 18-year-old self thought was a good idea at the time.

Maybe, in retrospect, the "People's Friend" is the only part that rings true, as I was just about to enter the most social phase of my life.

In 1978 I was at the University of New South Wales, studying Commerce and Law. I was meeting lots of smart new people. Also, fresh from an all-male high schooling, I was really enjoying being with women on a daily basis. (As it turns out, we get on great.) I was developing friendships with many interesting folk. Having been put through the regimentalism and relative homogeneity of a Christian Brothers education (about which, as an aside, I had no complaints at the time) ... I was ready to break loose.

I went out a LOT. Every night involved three or four different venues: pubs, bars and night clubs; meeting a bewildering diversity of people, including many strangers who tended to become intimate buddies by the early hours of the following morning. I was hungry for their stories, and often happy to become their fast friend.

At around this age I also used to spend a lot of time hanging out with a fun group of nurses at a share house in Paddington: Steve Lynch (the doctor who would later become a groomsman at my wedding), Genni Danesi (long since married to Steve), Jennifer Summerton (with whom, a few years later, I would enjoy a long-term relationship), Jane McCarthy, Anne d'Arbon and Maureen Boyle. They were high spirited and formative times.

When I look back on it now (tucked into bed straight after dinner, and watching episodes of *30 Rock* with Melanie), I marvel at that level of youthful stamina and social energy.

In the context of that time of my life, this business card made sense.

REMO GIUFFRE
Philosopher, Poet and People's Friend

24 Carrara Road,
Vaucluse 2030, NSW.   Ph: 337 1078

My business card, 1978

With Jane McCarthy and Maureen Boyle, 1978

1 2 3 4 5 6 7 8 9 10 11 12 13 14 15 16 17 18 19 20 21 22 23 24 25 26 27 28 29 30 31 32 33 34 35 36 37 38 39 40 41 42 43 44 45 46 47 48 49 50 51 52 53 54

1978

[11] Len Matchan & the Napkin Ring

When I was 19 and travelling on my own through Europe I stayed for a time on a tiny Channel Island near Guernsey called Brecqhou with the guy who both owned it and in fact technically *ruled* it, as a kingdom quite separate from the UK. He was a business associate of my father's. His name was Len Matchan, a self-made, but by then retired and very wealthy, cockney captain of industry.

Family legend has it that at six years of age, during one of Len's wining and dining trips to Sydney to check in on his businesses – Dad was his Deputy Chairman – I declared to Len's face that he was *"too fat and smoked too many cigars"* and that one day I was *"going to be a millionaire"* just like he was. (Well, at least I was right about the fat cigar guy bit.)

Anyway, back to 1979. I recall being collected in Jersey by a pilot who appeared to be wearing tails, and being ferried across to Brecqhou in Len's helicopter (branded with a coat of arms that appeared everywhere on Brecqhou). I was greeted by Len's partner Sue Groves. Sue had a parrot perched on her shoulder. His name was Hori. That, coupled with Sue's arthritic neck requiring her to tilt her head at an angle, made for quite an image.

And then this is what she said:

"Raymo [sic] ... it's soooo nice to have you here. Drop your bags and come with me. The King is waiting for you in the Snuggery."

And for four days I barely left that Snuggery. It was a quite a formative time, mentally jousting with Len all day and every day ... all the while Len drinking Bollinger Champagne or Tio Pepe sherry. He pushed, prodded and tested me about my hopes and aspirations, and there was a certain affection that developed between us. As an aside, he was horrified that I was studying law: *"How in Heaven's name is **that** going to help you read a balance sheet?"*

It helped that he had a deep respect for my father ... the only person who, in his view, could be relied on to speak the truth and stand up *strong* in the face of a Len Matchan board room barrage. He would tear up when he was telling me stories about Dad.

So, two years later back in Sydney, when I turned 21, it wasn't altogether surprising to receive this napkin ring in the mail.

It was interesting to see my name like that ... REMO in ALL CAPS, and I think that was maybe the first time I thought of my name as something potentially separate from myself.

At some level, Remo the person had been awakened to REMO the BRAND [30].

Len Matchan and the napkin ring

Len and Dad

Brecqhou, Channel Islands

Napkin ring
Brecqhou hallmarks

Brecqhou coat of
arms branded chopper

Brecqhou coat of
arms branded car

1 2 3 4 5 6 7 8 9 10 11 12 13 14 15 16 17 18 **19 20 21** 22 23 24 25 26 27 28 29 30 31 32 33 34 35 36 37 38 39 40 41 42 43 44 45 46 47 48 49 50 51 52 53 54
1979 1981

[12] The 1980 Aqua-Ball

I earned money as a student by working as a barman and wine waiter at a variety of establishments in Sydney's Eastern Suburbs. My most regular gig was at a function centre called the Orcades located at the very tip of Ben Buckler in North Bondi. It was owned and run by a colourful local named Barry Pillinger ("BP"), who once boasted to me that Liberace had offered to buy his premises for a million dollars. (As an aside, the building later became the Blue Water Grill, where Neil Perry first made his mark as a chef. Today it's a block of luxury apartments.)

In early 1980 I decided to organise a harbour cruise and to ask BP to provide the catering. I called it "The 1980 Aqua-Ball" and went about the planning and design of the elements: brand identity, food & beverage, entertainment offer, invitation copy, ticket sales strategy and break-even analysis. I ran an ad in a local Kings Cross paper doing a call out for buskers and had a wonderful time auditioning them all, ultimately settling on a burlesque entertainer named Fifi L'Amour (of whom I was already a fan), a male dancer, a drag queen and a rather odd chap who dressed as a pirate and played the spoons.

Tickets were priced at $15 each and the budget indicated that I needed to sell around 135 to break-even, but that if I sold 230 I could make over a thousand dollars in profit. I remember feeling exhilarated by the analysis and the magical potential to make a profit while having so much fun. So *this* is what it means to run your own business!

The most interesting thing I did, and surely my very first experiment with network marketing, was to break all of the tickets down into "Aqua-Packs" containing between 5 and 20 tickets each. Each pack was entrusted to a friend who became responsible for the marketing and sale of their allocation.

The cover letter that accompanied the ticket was designed to tantalise. Although somewhat clumsily written, it contained some language that would turn out to be a preview of my subsequent style as a wordsmith e.g.

"The 1980 Aqua-Ball will herald the beginning of a new concept in Harbour Cruises. Thongs and stubbies will be cast aside, and once again, elegance will be instilled into the moon-lit troughs and crests of Sydney Harbour."

Yikes. Thankfully, I improved as a copywriter.

Anyway, it all worked well enough. We sold 138 tickets, enough to break even; and everyone had a great night.

This was was my first thrilling taste of a truly soup-to-nuts experience design whereby I got to control every single element. It had been extremely satisfying for a 19/20-year-old commerce law student. I'd always been this way inclined, but now I had been bitten even harder by the entrepreneurial bug, and so my days as a member of the legal (or indeed any other) "profession" were probably numbered before they began.

THE 1980

AQUA-BALL

Saturday May 17th,1980

- The 1980 "Aqua-Ball" will herald the beginning of a new concept in Harbour Cruises. Thongs and stubbies will be cast aside, and once again, elegance will be instilled into the moon-lit troughs and crests of Sydney Harbour.

- The 4 hour cruise will be full of attractions never seen before on any Sydney Harbour ferry. The entertainment is varied,and should appeal to an extremely wide audience. It ranges from pleasantly eccentric tape music to Disc Jockey dancing music. As an added attraction,there will be a carnival atmosphere top deck which will be enhanced by the presence of talented Buskers - visual as well as audible.

- A bar will be manned by staff for the full 4 hours - serving keg beer, white wine and soft drink, without limit. The fact that tastes in spirits are so varied has meant that I have decided not to include such spirits in a package price

- The boat will stop briefly at the Watson's Ba

- The catering is being undertaken by M "Orcades Wedding Reception Centre".The a full one including hams, turkeys, ch 4 salads, etc., etc.

- The 1980 "Aqua-Ball" is an ambitious vent the best deal at an absolute minimum price from various sources has been overwhelming. you too will be able to participate in the 1

  Sincerely,

  REMO GIUFFRÈ

- Enquiries: Phone:337.1078

THE 1980

AQUA-BALL

TO BE HELD ON BOARD THE

M.V. PROCLAIM

8.00 p.m. - MIDNIGHT

SATURDAY, MAY, 17th 1980

(Leaving Wharf 6, Circular Quay)
at 8.00 p.m.

- TAPE MUSIC
- DISC JOCKEY
  LOWER DECK
- BUSKERS
  UPPER DECK
- DOOR PRIZE

Dress: Black Tie
and or Suave

- FULL SMORGASBORD
  SUPPER PROVIDED

- KEG BEER, WINE,
  SOFT DRINK
  PROVIDED ALL NIGHT

$15.00 Per Person
all inclusive

Aqua-Pack cover letter and sample ticket

MV Proclaim

Aqua-Pack Register

Break-even

With Jo Green
my then girlfriend

Fifi L'Amour
and friend

Dancer

Drag queen

Spoon playing pirate

Fun times

Anthony de Lorenzo
and Mark Kelly

1 2 3 4 5 6 7 8 9 10 11 12 13 14 15 16 17 18 19 20 21 22 23 24 25 26 27 28 29 30 31 32 33 34 35 36 37 38 39 40 41 42 43 44 45 46 47 48 49 50 51 52 53 54

1980

[13] The Weekender

My family owned a weekender at a place called Bayview to the north of Sydney. It was a single storey weatherboard shack with a great view down Pittwater all the way to Lion Island (named for its resemblance to a lion in sphinx position).

I spent many summers in that house, and on Atlanta, our wooden Halvorsen boat moored nearby. For me, both of those things became associated with time off and relaxation.

As we kids grew older, the weekender became less popular as a family holiday destination, and so Dad rented it out. A few years later, as a young adult, I became nostalgic about the weekender and began to yearn for it once more. So, I put a proposal to Dad. I would take on the lease myself, and pay him the rent, but on the condition that I could use the place as a club house.

That was the genesis of "The Weekender: a Club."

I wanted a place to escape to for the occasional weekend, and lots of my friends wanted the same thing. I was studying law at the time, so drafting up the rules would be good practice and straightforward, although some of the drafting to accommodate undisturbed 11th hour drop-in usage by horny couples became a bit contentious if I recall correctly.

The house became a haven, and on the occasional weekend a big group of us would be in residence. (I got to discover who of my friends were the loudest love makers. No names.)

The Weekender, like The Aqua-Ball [12] before it, and many things since, was a good example of my attraction to rule-making and community moderation. Indeed, here was yet another kingdom where I was able to create my own world, be in charge of that world, and not be subject to rules imposed by others.

Lion Island

Original Weekender artwork, 1982

The Weekender

Atlanta the Halvorsen

Club manual

The boss

Rules and regulations

Floorplans

Welcome letter

1 2 3 4 5 6 7 8 9 10 11 12 13 14 15 16 17 18 19 20 21 **22** 23 24 25 26 27 28 29 30 31 32 33 34 35 36 37 38 39 40 41 42 43 44 45 46 47 48 49 50 51 52 53 54

1982

[14] Crossing the Bridge

When I was 19 I had a crush on a fellow law student named Anne Davies. She liked me back … but not in that *special* way. It wasn't my first encounter with unrequited love, but it was happening at a time when I was burning the candle at both ends: trying to keep up at university, working a couple of jobs to pay rent on a share flat in Bronte, drinking, smoking, socialising a great deal, staying up very late … the usual young adult stuff.

One day I was driving my blue Mini across the Sydney Harbour Bridge to visit Anne at her family home in Longueville. At precisely the halfway point I had a panic attack. My heart started pounding, and it took all of my strength just to make it across safely to the other side.

I was exhausted and stressed, and this was how my body decided to let me know. Anyway, I got through the Anne thing (we became good friends), quit smoking, cut down on the drinking … and life returned to normal.

Fast forward four years to 1983. Now I'm at The College of Law [15], the campus for which happens to be on the other side of the Harbour Bridge from where I live (at that time in Edgecliff). And so, every day I'm driving across that bridge. Then one day something weird happens. My heart starts to race as I *approach* the bridge, only returning to normal as I emerge on the other side. Over time it gets worse. It starts to become debilitating, and so my brother Bruno the doctor refers me to a psychologist. The sessions delve into my history and explore my motivations. What becomes apparent is this:

My experience at The College of Law was making me realise that a legal career track was the wrong one for me, and that was making me *very anxious*. Due to its starring role in my panic attack at 19, the Sydney Harbour Bridge had become a *symbol* upon which I was focusing my generalised anxieties. Each time I crossed the bridge I was having a parasympathetic reaction born of the previous physiological attack. OK.

The treatment proposed was "systematic desensitisation" whereby I would gradually coax myself into becoming a confident bridge crosser again. I tried that, and for a while I was making progress. I even had a relaxing Vanuatu holiday snap of myself pinned to the underside of the sun visor. But to no avail. Not only was I unable to cure the Sydney Harbour Bridge phobia, it actually extended over time to include: other bridges, tunnels and driving on highways. Even heights. Meanwhile, life was hurtling forward, and I had many things that I wanted to do. So basically I decided to put my "gephyrophobia" into the too hard basket and just learn to avoid those situations that were going to cause me discomfort. Possibly not textbook stuff and I don't necessarily recommend it.

Even today, I don't like bridges or driving. I have a licence but very rarely use it. Thankfully, Melanie is a good and keen driver. Another reason why we're such a great life match? I've learned to live with those fears by not dealing with them. Courage comes in many forms … and this is not a battle that I have thus far chosen to pick.

The experience has made me aware of the fragility of the human psyche and what can happen when one pushes things too hard or too far. It really is useful to understand your limits and to know where your edges live.

Sydney Harbour Bridge opening, 19 March 1932

With Anne Davies, 1979

Blue Mini

The College of Law [15]

Sunbaking in Vanuatu
The Relaxation Image

Only if I really have to …

1 2 3 4 5 6 7 8 9 10 11 12 13 14 15 16 17 18 19 20 21 22 23 24 25 26 27 28 29 30 31 32 33 34 35 36 37 38 39 40 41 42 43 44 45 46 47 48 49 50 51 52 53 54

1979   1983

[15] Quentin Steele

The College of Law is a place in Sydney where newly graduating lawyers go to spend six months as a member of a pretend law firm learning about the practicalities of work as a solicitor in New South Wales. The curriculum is pitched to the general practitioner who is basically doing everything: conveyancing, personal injury cases, wills, contracts, and so on.

By the time I started at The College of Law in 1983, I had already accepted an offer for full-time employment from Baker & McKenzie, a global law firm with a dynamic office in Sydney. The focus at Baker & McKenzie was corporate, and so I knew that I wasn't going to be needing a lot of the knowledge that The College was designed to deliver.

For that reason, and possibly also due to the fact that in my heart I already knew that the legal path was not the right one for me, I *detested* that experience with a passion. My levels of boredom were only matched by the frustration and resentment I felt about all of the bureaucratic procedures that we were being asked to learn.

Enter Quentin Steele, that *"serious yet idealistic young professional."*

I had been the cartoonist at Law School, and here again I had quickly fallen into the role of college cartoonist, encouraged by my good friend Bob Fox, who was editing the weekly college newsletter. Quentin was the hero of a cartoon strip that appeared in that newsletter. He was the rebellious cynic that I was possibly too chicken to be in real life. He *hated* it there at college and poured scorn onto the system on a weekly basis. I got to vent and live vicariously through Quentin. It was an outlet for me that made the experience tolerable.

Quentin became a cult hero at The College of Law. His weekly "College Capers" were followed closely, not just by us inmates, but also by our procedure-obsessed overseers. Quentin was a member of Club Delta (spiritually reformed in New York as Club Niche [18] a couple of years later). Finally, there was an underground market for a range of Club Delta T Shirts bearing Quentin's image. He was pretty pleased about that too.

So far, so good … in terms of Quentin's cult status and rebelliousness cred.

But come graduation day, the whole thing backfired. We were all individually presented with certificates to mark our passage through The College. I collected mine and returned to my seat. When they got down to the S's, Quentin's name was read out; which meant that I had to return to the podium to collect one on "his" behalf. The College had co-opted my character, and what had been an underground thing was all of a sudden just another part of the system.

As Quentin would say: *"Sheesh!"*

Complete set of strips presented to The College on graduation day, 24 June 1983

The Complete
Qentin Steele

Collection of
weekly strips

Club Delta stamp

Club Delta T Shirt
at The Weekender [13]

Quentin Steele's
graduation certificate

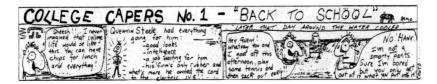

1 2 3 4 5 6 7 8 9 10 11 12 13 14 15 16 17 18 19 20 21 22 23 24 25 26 27 28 29 30 31 32 33 34 35 36 37 38 39 40 41 42 43 44 45 46 47 48 49 50 51 52 53 54

1983

[16] MemoRandom

Baker & McKenzie is today the world's largest law firm, employing 4,100 lawyers in 75 offices and 47 countries. Its global coverage is unique. Even so, back in 1982, when I was interviewing with the firm, it was not the first choice for some of my high-achieving law school colleagues. For those interested in the more traditional big city Sydney firms such as Allen Allen & Hemsley or Freehill Hollingdale & Page, Chicago-based Baker & McKenzie was regarded as a bit brash and somewhat of an outlier ... which is just how I liked it.

Baker & McKenzie's Sydney office had a corporate law focus, which also suited me fine. Six months at The College of Law [15] was more than enough time to teach me that I had absolutely no interest in the nitty gritty of a suburban practice. I ended up working on a range of corporate matters and became the firm's Foreign Investment Review Board ("FIRB") specialist, which meant that I was involved in lots of proposed mergers and acquisitions.

Thrilling for some ... but nothing to get *my* heart racing.

I was more interested in the dynamic of the workplace; and that's when I decided to propose something to the partners. I would edit a new weekly newsletter designed to inform, amuse and unite a firm that was growing fast and finding it hard to maintain a unified culture.

MemoRandom was born.

Every week I would gather office news and ephemera and package it up into an appealing two pager. On Thursdays it would be printed and distributed. My favourite thing in the world at the time was to pace all three floors of the office and drink in the sight of every single person stopping to read their copy of *MemoRandom*. I was responsible for an experience that everyone shared. That felt powerful. I liked that feeling.

And, in retrospect, I have to tip my hat to Baker & McKenzie. In terms of billable hours, my productivity left much to be desired. More often than not, I drew smiley faces on my time sheets. Not only did they tolerate this, they actually nurtured and encouraged me in my self-appointed job as internal editor/publisher. They let me create a role that didn't exist before. That was smart and wise, and I repaid that wisdom with lots of good karma and happy vibes. *MemoRandom* became another reason for top graduates to choose Baker & McKenzie.

Flexible, tolerant and far-sighted employers always win in the end.

PS: Years later, inspired by *MemoRandom*, I would name the REMO newsletter *RemoRandom*.

Selection of Baker & McKenzie MemoRanda, 1983–1984

Job offer, 1982   With Bob Fox and the FIRB manual   My proposal to partners   Face fax cartoon   RemoRandom

REMO GIUFFRÉ

ATTORNEY & SOLICITOR

BAKER & McKENZIE
A M P CENTRE   TEL 231 5488
50 BRIDGE STREET   TELEX 21618
SYDNEY AUSTRALIA   CABLE ABOGADO

Business card, 1983   My final day at B&McK time sheet

1 2 3 4 5 6 7 8 9 10 11 12 13 14 15 16 17 18 19 20 21 22 **23** 24 25 26 27 28 29 30 31 32 33 34 35 36 37 38 39 40 41 42 43 44 45 46 47 48 49 50 51 52 53 54

1983

[17] The Castanet Club

In 1983 I was working as a corporate lawyer at Baker & McKenzie [16]; but I was also on the books as a volunteer for the Arts Law Centre, founded and headed by Shane Simpson who, incidentally, would go on to become the lawyer for REMO General Store [25].

One day Shane called to tell me that he had a gig that he felt would interest me. There was a troupe of young cabaret performers in Newcastle (north of Sydney) who required some legal advice. I was to head up there to meet with them and figure out what they needed. So, the following weekend I took the train up the coast and was greeted at the station by The Castanet Club administrator Jodi Shields (who would go on to become the first REMO General Manager). Jodi drove me to the hotel and checked me in, prepaying for my room with a handful of crumpled bank notes extracted from various pockets. I was embarrassed by the gesture. I could've and should've been sleeping on someone's couch. I certainly didn't feel like a lawyer from the big smoke, but I was being treated like that.

I met the crew and we bonded very quickly. Their performance that night was extraordinary. There was real magic in what they were doing. It was palpable and undeniable. My enthusiasm was rewarded with friendship and trust. That's me in the Santa suit with the band on that very day. Their regular Santa didn't show. So they asked their newly minted lawyer to don the red and white.

I was able to sell the The Castanet Club in to Baker & McKenzie as a pro bono client (under the watchful gaze of partner Jennifer Wilson). They moved to Sydney and delighted audiences for years with their unique blend of music and humour. Their success culminated in 1990 with a film directed by Neil Armfield and produced by Glenys Rowe (both REMO customers). It was filmed over the course of two performances at the North Bondi RSL. If you're ever curious enough to see it, you might even see me in the audience, sitting with Katy Foster [65], smiling from ear to ear and proud as punch.

The Castanet Club generated a fanatically loyal following and created a sense of family that has outlived the life of the band by many years. Their alumni list of members and close collaborators reads like a who's who of the Australian media and entertainment industry.

As with REMO, there's also a sense that The Castanet Club could have gone further and become bigger. Imagine The Wiggles, but smart, funny and appealing to adults. I think that a couple of the members of the band feel that melancholic sense of missed opportunity sometimes, as do I with REMO, and maybe that's another reason why I feel so close to those guys. We share something bittersweet, in that we both touched and delighted a lot of people, made a big cultural impact, and yet found it difficult in the end to make our creation financially sustainable.

Mikey for REMO, clearing the
previous tenant's stock, 1988

Remo as Santa with The Castanet Club, December 1983

The film

REMO Crown Street Window [44], April 1991

The Castanet Club

Jodi   Steve   Glenn   Rodney   Russell   Warren   Angela   Maynard   Lana   Penny   Kathy   Mikey

SUBSEQUENTLY REMO GENERAL STORE [25] ALUMNI

1 2 3 4 5 6 7 8 9 10 11 12 13 14 15 16 17 18 19 20 21 22 23 24 25 26 27 28 29 30 31 32 33 34 35 36 37 38 39 40 41 42 43 44 45 46 47 48 49 50 51 52 53 54

1983

[18] Club Niche

Ivy League Business Schools tend to be fairly serious places and Columbia Business School in the City of New York is no exception. Lots of ambitious Americans on their postgraduate paths to glory, and a smattering of usually wealthy international students rubbing shoulders with the Americans and looking to get ahead.

Business school can also be a fairly *earnest* environment; which is why I co-founded Club Niche in cahoots with a New Yorker and ex-band manager named Daniel Savage. Club Niche was formed to satirise Business School. We formed it in late 1984, soon after the commencement of our first term.

The foundation members of Club Niche were a dozen or so fellow MBA students, both American and international (Damien, Dan, Ann, Liz, Susan, Duccio, Mark, Simon, Joe – you know who you are), all of whom, like me, felt a bit different and maybe a little bit less serious than some of the Wall Street bankers and Madison Avenue wankers.

We used to meet at local bars and restaurants and gather around a centrepiece that was a battery operated moving hand (holding a flag bearing the red letter "N") emerging from a hole in an upside down shoe box, upon which were stuck name badge stickers, once again bearing the red letter "N." During our sessions we all wore one of those "N" badges as a mark of solidarity and to intrigue any other people in the bar.

The *raison d'être* of Club Niche was simply to *be*. We didn't do much at all … except meet, eat, drink … and maybe tease all of the people who *weren't* in Club Niche.

It was interesting, however, how the formation of the club served to bring kindred spirits together quickly. Put it this way: if I was hand-picking members for the club after two full years of peer group observation, I would have included *all* of the people who somehow managed to connect with it (in some cases via word of mouth) within the first two *weeks*.

At the end of our two years together we chopped the ceremonial rubber hand (referred to as "the conch") into pieces, and each senior member of Club Niche got to take a piece home.

The experience taught me, yet again, that like-mindedness and kinship is out there for all of us, and that it only ever requires someone (or in this case some *thing*) to fly the flag.

Inaugural meeting of Club Niche, New York City, 11 October 1984

1 2 3 4 5 6 7 8 9 10 11 12 13 14 15 16 17 18 19 20 21 22 23 24 25 26 27 28 29 30 31 32 33 34 35 36 37 38 39 40 41 42 43 44 45 46 47 48 49 50 51 52 53 54

1984 - 1986

[19] Stalking Rupert Murdoch

At some point during the second year of my MBA studies at Columbia Business School in 1985 I became obsessed about working with Rupert Murdoch. #

Media and communications had become "my thing," and I'd even crafted my own customised "Communications Management" major at B School by cross-registering for subjects in the Schools of Journalism and the Arts. At every opportunity my MBA field work involved companies operating in that "space" there in Manhattan: Dow Jones, HBO, the New York Post, PAPER Magazine and others. Total immersion.

News Corporation had acquired 20th Century Fox and had just announced its purchase of the Metromedia group of independent television stations, setting the stage for the launch of a fourth US commercial broadcasting network, something that the "experts" had been saying for a long time was impossible (but which my own final year thesis had argued was do-able). Rupert was well and truly on the move in the US, playing by his own rules and ruffling all sorts of establishment feathers. As an outsider myself, and an Australian to boot, I found it fun to watch.

The maverick in me was attracted to the ascendancy of this alpha maverick, and so I set about working on ways to hitch my wagon to that star. I had mixed success to begin with. Like most MBA students I did a summer internship between my first and second years of study. My internship was with Murdoch Magazines. At Rupert's suggestion I did end up doing *"some real work somewhere under Marty Singerman"* at the offices of *New York Magazine*. (One of the perks of the internship was a free personal ad, but that's a whole other story.) It wasn't a great experience. I didn't really fit the profile of the unquestioning loyalist to the Sun King, and I think that Marty and the other loyal lieutenants thought of me as a bit too interested in my own ideas and opinions. (However, I did meet my then girlfriend Heather Martin there; so that was one good thing.)

This less than ideal experience didn't put me off working with Rupert, but I decided that I'd be better off working directly with the man himself. So, I spent much of late 1985 plotting my pitch to become his right-hand MBA. I was thorough … schmoozing both of his PAs, Dorothy "Dot" Wyndoe and Paige M. (I even took Paige to lunch and received coaching from the inside.) I eventually got them to schedule the meeting with Rupert, and I felt confident that I was going to be able to sell him the idea face to face. That's when fate intervened. I received the news that my father was close to death [6]. A hastily booked flight home to Sydney meant that I was going to have to postpone the meeting. Life took some more twists and turns, and that meeting was not rescheduled.

I realise now that my Rupert obsession was never going to have a happy ending. There was only ever room for one Sun King on that mountain, and for me to be able to be me as a player and communicator at any level, I was going to have to start my own mole hill.

At the time I was also identifying with Howard Roark and Hank Reardon, the unashamedly individualistic heroes of Ayn Rand's *Fountainhead* and *Atlas Shrugged*, so it made some sense.

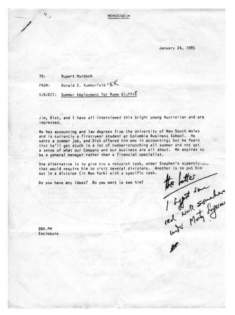

MEMORANDUM

January 24, 1985

TO: Rupert Murdoch

FROM: Donald D. Kummerfeld

SUBJECT: Summer Employment for Remo Giuffré

Jim, Dick, and I have all interviewed this bright young Australian and are impressed.

He has accounting and law degrees from the University of New South Wales and is currently a first-year student at Columbia Business School. He wants a summer job, and Dick offered him one in accounting; but he fears that he'll get stuck in a lot of number-crunching all summer and not get a sense of what our Company and our business are all about. He aspires to be a general manager rather than a financial specialist.

One alternative is to give him a research task, under Stephen's supervision, that would require him to visit several divisions. Another is to put him out in a division (in New York) with a specific task.

Do you have any ideas? Do you want to see him?

DDK.PM
Enclosure

Remo Giuffré
207 Second Avenue, #4
New York, N.Y., 10003
Tel: (212) 777 - 8786

Mr. Rupert Murdoch
210 South Street,
New York, New York 10002

28 October, 1985.

Dear Mr. Murdoch,

My name is Remo Giuffré and, partly at your instigation, I worked at New York magazine over this past summer. I am Australian and am here in New York completing some post-graduate studies at Columbia University.

Although our paths have yet to cross, I have had considerable contact with some other senior people in your organisation: - Sir James Cruthers, Don Kummerfeld, Nick Lloyd, Dick Sarazen and John Evans - to name a few.

I would like to work full-time for you, upon the completion of my studies. Having closely examined the marketplace, I have come to the conclusion that my own personal style, energies and "culture" would find their closest and best fit with the positioning and culture of News Corp. worldwide.

Needless to say, I am keenly interested in News Corp's present and proposed business activities. I feel strongly that the organisation is uniquely positioned in this and other markets to take full advantage of the fast evolving communications environment.

I propose a specific and carefully considered (admittedly ideal) scenario. Enclosed is an outline of: - what I propose, what I feel I have to offer, and how I think I can add real value to your business. Also enclosed is a condensed form of my resume.

I realise that it might be some time before you have the chance to focus on this matter. Even so, I would be keen to discuss it in person with you when your schedule permits.

Yours Sincerely,

Remo Giuffré

CC : Sir James Cruthers

Memo and response from Rupert, 24 January 1985

Proposal to Rupert, 28 October 1985

Rupert Murdoch

Fourth TV Network Issue Analysis, 1985

Making a point at *New York Magazine*

KRM proposal October 1985

See [82]

1 2 3 4 5 6 7 8 9 10 11 12 13 14 15 16 17 18 19 20 21 22 23 24 25 26 27 28 29 30 31 32 33 34 35 36 37 38 39 40 41 42 43 44 45 46 47 48 49 50 51 52 53 54

1985

[20] Communicating Guy

I have been a communicating guy for a long time. Since 1970 is just a guess.

An early manifestation of this show-off gene was note passing in class at school. I could spend a whole lesson scribbling wisecracks and waiting for responses.

At some point I decided that one-to-one communication was OK but that one-to-many might be more fun, and time saving to boot. So that's when I started with the photocopied form letters to friends and more ambitious projects like MemoRandom [16]. My friends got used to receiving form letters from me when I was studying in New York, and I perfected a casual warts'n'all style of communication that made people feel that I was writing just to them. It wasn't forced or fake. It's what I really felt.

One-to-many become one-to-many-**more** when I was driving customer communications at the REMO General Store [25]. The REMO mailing list grew from 1,500 when we got started in 1988 to around 100,000 in 1995. Once or twice a year I got the chance to communicate with **all** of these customers, and once again the writing style was conversational and direct. Also, the catalogues were very text heavy, and all of the "industry experts" were at pains to tell me how wrong it all was, and that people didn't want to read that much stuff … but of course they did, because what I was writing was (I think) interesting and genuine, and not just generic filler or marketing spin.

And then the Internet happened … and, along with it, email. That's when my customer missives could (and did) become more frequent … maybe *too* frequent. Even during the most miserable we're-on-the-verge-of-going-broke-again times during the most recent version of REMO, it was never a chore to sit down and write to customers. I love to tell people what's happening and I like those words to include what I genuinely *feel*.

Finally, this book is another example of where I can be myself and write as I talk. (I know that's what I do, because I often catch myself speaking aloud what I've written.)

In a 1991 feature article in Australia's *HQ* magazine, journalist Patty Huntington was of the view that: *"Communication is clearly Remo Giuffre's great gift."*

Maybe she was right.

PS: There is, by the way, a downside to being a communicating guy. I've had to learn, often the hard way, what can and can't be forwarded via email, and to whom. My tendency has always been to let everyone know about everything, and that's not always the right thing to do.

REMO, MELANIE & LOLA GIUFFRÉ
4/124 RAMSGATE AVENUE BONDI BEACH SYDNEY 2026
TEL: (02) 365 5941 • FAX: (02) 365 0286 • EMAIL: remo@remo.com.au

SATURDAY 6 APRIL 1996

AN UPDATE FOR OUR FRIENDS FROM
REMO & MELANIE & LOLA

Dear

This is a form letter. (As if you couldn't tell.)

There's just so much that you can squeeze on to a single page of an A6 Christmas card. Therefore, I convinced Melanie that it would be a good idea for me to spend Easter Saturday morning downstairs here in the dank home office pounding away on this UPDATE rather than helping her force yoghurt-like substances down our daughter Lola's sometimes smiling but sometimes screaming face. (She's getting over a cold virus and is still not quite herself. It's the very first time that she's been sick since she was born.)

This type of letter comes very naturally to me. When I was living in New York I kept in touch with my friends in Australia by handwriting (complete with photos and illustrations) long bulletins that I proceeded to photocopy and send to more than 60 different places. This letter is being sent to a fraction of that number; however the principle is the same – ramble on and don't spend too much time trying to introduce structure or even sense.

Anyway, on to the UPDATE.

Two things have deeply influenced our lives this past year: my business ("REMO") and our daughter ("Lola") – not necessarily in that order.

REMO RECAP

"Sweet are the uses of adversity."
•
WILLIAM SHAKESPEARE

1995/96 was a year of significant hardship and struggle for the business and consequently for Melanie and me personally. After several years of sustained growth, REMO hit a speed bump (euphemism) and was forced to deal with its mounting debt. A "white knight" in the form of a Melbourne based retail operator emerged in July 1995 and then promptly collapsed himself just this past January 1996 (for reasons other than REMO).

Letter to friends and family, 6 April 1996

| Postcard February 2002 | RemoRandom | Communicating Guy 1991 | General Thinking Newsletter | HQ *Magazine*, 1991 |

1 2 3 4 5 6 7 8 9 10 11 12 13 14 15 16 17 18 19 20 21 22 23 24 25 26 27 28 29 30 31 32 33 34 35 36 37 38 39 40 41 42 43 44 45 46 47 48 49 50 51 52 53 54

1970 ← → 2014

[21] Fish Head

It's due to Fish Head that I met my good friend Dare Jennings.

In 1985 Dare, who these days oversees the international expansion of the Deus Ex Machina brand, was just getting started on his first act, the iconic and now 30-year-old MAMBO brand. My friend Wayne Golding was the art director there.

Dare took a shine to my drawing of a severed fish head (with a bulbous eye that made said fish look suspiciously like Quentin Steele [15]). Wayne made the introduction and Dare, who was travelling through New York, came to see me in my SoHo studio in 1986. We did the belated deal, and Fish Head was added to the embryonic MAMBO designs range.

When I returned to Sydney in 1987 I connected with Dare, who was also living in Bondi [23]. We became friends and remain close. He is my daughter Lola's godfather [67].

In 2008 *The Weekend Australian* magazine featured the two of us in a "Double Take" piece where we both got to describe the genesis and dynamic of our relationship.

He said: *"Remo is an eccentric, passionate person ... [REMO General Store] was hugely successful. It was completely revolutionary, a shop not just for one product, but for all the things he was interested in. I guess we both had similar ideas about creating brands that were cultural experiences. But we did it in a different way. My thing with MAMBO was to take ideas from a collective of artists, whereas Remo's brand was based on his own personality."*

And I said: *"The way I see it, Dare and I belong to the old entrepreneurs' club. We have both committed most of our lives to developing our own brands. We've both been controlling our destinies for a long time, and we've lost the taste for any less control. But he's been better at turning his ideas into cash ... Like me, he doesn't see his work and his life as two separate things ... I guess ours is a kind of fraternal relationship. I look at him as an older brother, someone who has been around the block a couple more times than I have."*

Given our similarities and shared interests, it's a fair bet that Dare and I would have connected even if Fish Head hadn't come along. However, it's interesting to ponder how things may have been different, had that been the case.

Life is a series of chance meetings, connections made and opportunities taken.

Photo: Andy Baker

Mambo founder **Dare Jennings**, 57, and **Remo Giuffre**, 47, of the Remo General Store talk to *Drew Warne-Smith* about a friendship that's flourished in hard times.

The Weekend Australian, February 2008

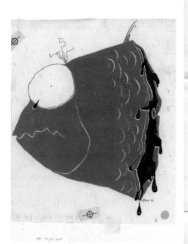

Artwork separated for printing

436 West Broadway, Apt. 10L
New York, N.Y. 10012
(212) 966 - 5466

Dare Jennings
Mambo Graphics Pty.Ltd.
62-74 Botany Rd. Alexandria,
2015, N.S.W. Australia   21 September, 1986

→ Mum etc

Mum,
Pls show
Jo-anne
next
time
She's
over
I think
she'd
be
intereste
Remo

Dear Dare,

I enjoyed meeting with you the other day. Wayne had often talked of his entrepreneurial boss. I'm delighted that you are interested in using some of my designs in your garment lines. Nothing excites me more than the prospect of spotting one of my babies on a beach next time I'm in Oz.

Wayne's note cleared up the minor confusion regarding "fish-head". Apparently he made an "executive decision" to authorise the reproduction, leaving us to "thrash out the financial terms" later. He made the right decision.

The Designs

• So far, you seem interested in "fish-head", "rubber chicken" and maybe "sushi". As you could see, I have developed 20 to 30 new designs, some of which I'm hoping may be attractive to the urban Manhattan market. (You saw the start of my mail order effort.) I will send you and Wayne a photocopy of everything I do for your perusal. I welcome any feedback and am not averse to designing something to specifications if desired.

• I like your yardage concept **very much**. As I understand it, you wish to print patterns that appear from afar to be standard, innocuous and Hawaiian but which close up reveal themselves to be surprising, bizarre and offbeat. "Fish-head" and "rubber chicken" are clearly appropriate. Think also about the "Bitey" design and a cockroach motif. Finally, think especially hard about the sushi idea. A yardage print of different sushi pieces could be made to look standard from afar yet <u>very strange</u> at close range - the perfect combination! This design is in progress. Please notify.

The Arrangement

☐ In short, I am 100% happy about you merchandising my designs. My only concerns appear to be the standard ones. That is, that: • My designs appear as intended and substantially unaltered, • My name appears next to the ● on each and every design rendition, and that • My $ reward is tied closely to the marketing and sales success of the garments bearing my designs.

Letter to Dare, 21 September 1986

Sketch

Fish Head as a MAMBO design
1985

Rubber Chicken
rejected

*The Weekend
Australian*, 2008

[22] It's Our Pleasure to Serve You

I experienced my first taste of real design success as a 25 year old living in New York.

I was halfway through my postgraduate MBA studies at Columbia Business School. I didn't live near the university, but rather in a share house in the East Village (above what was then something called *Noodle House,* and which is currently the *momofuku ssäm bar*). I lived with Carl Størmer, a Norwegian drummer, and Julie Wolsk, a dancer/ choreographer from Copenhagen. I was studying and living an exciting and relatively edgy life on the Lower East Side. For period atmospherics think: the Palladium and Area nightclubs, Andy Warhol, Grace Jones, Talking Heads and Keith Haring.

I had long been fascinated by the ubiquity and "Greekness" of the iconic NYC takeout coffee cup, and I thought it would make a great T shirt design. There were a few versions of the cup out there, and I cherry picked my favourite features of each. I hand drew the design and shopped it around to a few of the funkier stores in my neighbourhood. That's when I met Jon Millstein and Emily Clarke at Design East. They only sold T shirts bearing their own ideas. However, they became so enamoured with my take out cup design that they licensed it from me and started producing, and selling it, and paying me some royalties.

Some years later when I launched the REMO General Store [25] in Sydney, I included the design within our launch portfolio; and it remained in the range for many years.

I stumble across T shirts bearing the design for sale here and there and from time to time, and not only the Design East version. I'm not sure how this has happened, nor do I really care too much about any unpaid royalties. You can spend a lot of time worrying about that stuff, and I'm just as happy to see my work out there.

The last time I saw a T shirt in a New York store bearing the design, I was pleased to see that my name was still there as part of the print; and I'm grateful for that attribution.

© Remo Giuffrè 1985

The cup

Original artwork

Janet and Cheryle at REMO in 1988

With Jon and Emily at Design East NYC, 1989

Tokyo store display

1 2 3 4 5 6 7 8 9 10 11 12 13 14 15 16 17 18 19 20 21 22 23 24 25 26 27 28 29 30 31 32 33 34 35 36 37 38 39 40 41 42 43 44 45 46 47 48 49 50 51 52 53 54

1985

[23] Bondi Beach

I've always been strongly attracted to Bondi, and in particular the beach. I did most of my schooling in the neighbourhood at Waverley College [4], and even though as a kid I spent much of my actual beach time closer to our Kensington home at Maroubra, Bondi has always been part of the bigger picture.

When, having completed my MBA studies, I returned to Sydney from New York in 1987, I frankly couldn't understand why anyone would want to live anywhere else other than in this utopia. A few years away from Sydney and living within the density of Manhattan had made me appreciate the uniqueness of a place where the natural beauty of an ever-changing ocean meets an urban environment so effortlessly. (As an aside, this kind of thinking and banging on about Bondi is associated with what is referred to by the locals as living in the "Bondi Bubble" and is justifiably a source of great irritation for anybody in Sydney who doesn't live, or aspire to live, in Bondi.)

Such is my allegiance to the neighbourhood that in 2008 I paid homage to Bondi on a full page of the REMO Printed Thing [72]. That page is reproduced in full here. Some of the locals featured on that page have moved on … but the spirit remains the same.

Melanie and I have lived near the beach in Bondi on and off for a long time now, and it's hard for us to imagine living anywhere else [80]. It has also been a great place to raise a family. Both of our kids are anchored here. Roman is especially "baked-on Bondi," spending most of his time either in the ocean or at the skate park. In fact he's become such a local that the artist Jeremyville incorporated Roman into the mural that adorns the walls of the Messina Gelato outpost on Hall Street.

So what's the point?

For me this is about finding out where you really *belong* … and the luck of when that place turns out to be amazing.

Photo: Sobo Image

Roman riding finless

Jeremyville mural
Messina Gelato Bondi

2008 | Bondi Beach | 14 July 2007

The Hotel Bondi

Flag and Surfers

Nina at Ploy Thai

Bondi Surf Club

Kolby at NBIF

Noel at IDRB

Visual Homage

There are prettier beachside communities, but there's something about Bondi that gets under your skin and stays there. (Not everybody feels this way, but we do.) There are lots of obvious reasons for the visceral appeal of the beach: stunningly beautiful setting, great swimming and snorkeling, iconic Bondi Pavilion, strong local community, urban proximity, lots of authentic retail; but we reckon that the most appealing thing about Bondi is the bewildering diversity of the people who live around or frequent the beach on any given day.

At any one time you might encounter: pods of local surfers, groovy skate boys, bus loads of Korean tourists, well oiled muscle men toning their bodies, capoeira instructors trying their best to look fearsome, briny guys in speedos sizzling sausages, families at the north end, fashionistas, boot campers, life savers, kite flyers, hippies, rev-heads, schoolies, artists, old people, young people, fat people, skinny people ... every race and nationality imaginable.

Enjoy our visual homage to Bondi.

All photographs taken between 11am & 3pm on Saturday 14 July 2007.

Ben at the Bergs

Uge at Aquabumps

John Macarthur

Ice Cream Van

North Bondi

Squeekie Bill at the Tratt

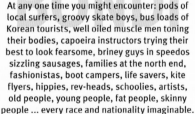
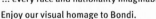
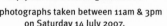
Bondi Merchandise at /BONDI

Caroline at Bondi Organic

Gabe at Sean's

Andy at Sejuiced

Skate Boarders

The Book Shop

Melanie at the Bergs

WWW.REMOGENERALSTORE.COM/**BONDI**

REMO Printed Thing 2008, Page 174

1 2 3 4 5 6 7 8 9 10 11 12 13 14 15 16 17 18 19 20 21 22 23 24 25 26 27 28 29 30 31 32 33 34 35 36 37 38 39 40 41 42 43 44 45 46 47 48 49 50 51 52 53 54

1987 ◄──────► 1997   2002 ◄──────► 2014

[24] Searching for the Idea

I'm the kind of person who needs a project and a goal, but I also need to feel that the underlying *idea* is worthy of my undiluted focus.

For a course that I was taking at the Columbia Journalism School as part of my MBA studies in 1985, I developed the idea for a printed magazine called *RECAP* that would be a weekly digest of news and opinions snipped from a curated selection of media titles. It was a parasitic media idea designed for the time-poor professional looking to be across the essence of the week without having to do a whole lot of reading. Meh.

A bigger obsession was my idea for a weekly news poster called *WALLPAPER*. I started working on that in 1986 while I was still living in New York. I was inspired at the time by Chris Whittle who was deploying lots of wall media out there into medical waiting rooms and college dorms. But my idea was more urban … and was no doubt inspired by my internship at *New York Magazine*, and also by my early personal publishing experiences with *College Capers* [15] and *MemoRandom* [16]. *WALLPAPER* was envisioned to be a framed and oversized one-page poster that would inform, entertain and inspire the citizenry while they were going about the business of living in the metropolis: travelling in elevators, waiting on queues, standing at bus shelters, and so on … I really thought that this was going to be THE idea into which I would be pouring my considerable creative and business energies. I was taking meetings and getting some traction.

But it was not to be. For whatever reason, one day I woke up and it didn't feel like THE idea any more; and I remember being extremely disoriented by that realisation. So much so that, and for the second time in my life, I sought help by going to see a psychotherapist. As it happens, I think my decision may have had more to do with my father's recent death [6] and a desire to reconnect with my Sydney roots [61], than it had to do with my perception of the quality of *WALLPAPER* as an idea. (Ten years later a Canadian journalist named Tyler Brûlé would use *Wallpaper** as the name for a more traditional magazine.)

The coolest thing about REMO [25] is that for such a long time it was so unequivocally THE idea for me, which meant that no amount of time spent working on it was wasted. Once that idea had qualified in my mind as THE idea, it benefited from a staggering amount of my focus. When I look back at all of the intellectual property manifest in that award-winning November 1991 catalogue [43], I see the groundwork laid for just about every other idea that followed in the next 15 years.

The right idea is worth searching for. Keep searching and you will eventually find something that qualifies. If it involves something that you love [7], and that you also happen to be good at, that's great. You are in the right place.

PS: In February 1990 I faxed Tibor Kalman [47] to tell him about another new BIG idea, "*REMO*" magazine: "*National Geographic without the topless natives & corn millet, but chock-a-block full of things that **interest** people who live in **cities** – 'mondo cane' with a twist.*" The following year he became the founding editor of *Colors* magazine for Benetton, "*a magazine about the rest of the world.*" Different but similar. Just saying. Tibor and I often good-naturedly accused one another of "brain invasion."

WALLPAPER mockup, New York City, 1986

This 1986 note to self identifies seven quite different career options for me post-MBA: fine artist, designer/artist, design house and consultancy, start-up publisher, media acquirer, employed media executive and a consultant who takes equity stakes. I ended up back in Sydney and worked as a media executive for about six months (Director of Business Development for Network Film Corporation Limited), before quitting to work full time on the launch of REMO.

1 2 3 4 5 6 7 8 9 10 11 12 13 14 15 16 17 18 19 20 21 22 23 24 25 26 27 28 29 30 31 32 33 34 35 36 37 38 39 40 41 42 43 44 45 46 47 48 49 50 51 52 53 54

1986

[25] REMO General Store

REMO was launched in Sydney in 1988 as a General Store with a mission to serve and delight a global network of involved customers; to celebrate quality and passion in people and merchandise gathered together from all over the world.

So, what gave me the idea?

I had always been interested in self-expressive design, but also very keen to run my own business. For a long time these two drivers were at odds. The visually creative side of me got channelled into things like cartooning and clubs, while the business side got fed by my formal studies and early experiences as a lawyer and wannabe media executive.

The tension between these two passions was resolved when I figured out that the way to combine them was to be *in the **business** of communicating design and **passion***. Eureka!

That was the genesis of the REMO General Store and the reason why it developed so quickly and attracted so much attention. Once the previously perpendicular forces of business and creative design became more parallel in alignment, things *really* took off. The momentum was obvious to everybody.

It's not what I was initially expecting. The decision to launch REMO was a lifestyle decision born of my aversion to corporate life and my desperate desire to live a life of passion. Some friends and family were initially quite confused. Says Mum at the time: *"Darling, you've got three degrees, and you're opening a shop. Please help me understand."*

I thought it might turn out to be a small life, but for the reasons given here and elsewhere, it actually turned out to be quite a big life; although not one without its ups and downs.

Here is my REMO story in a nutshell:

I opened a store with a focus on quality and passion. We produced great catalogues. We attracted a lot of attention from all over the world. We ran out of money. We went broke, ironically at the peak of our popularity (ouch!). We went into hibernation for a few years. We came back online to finish what we started. We did that for 10 years, before running out of money again in 2012. We wound down the retail, and put the brand back on ice.

That's nearly 24 years of REMO history ... which feels like enough for the time being.

It was a fun ride that I feel honoured to have shared with so many great customers.

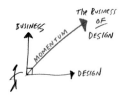

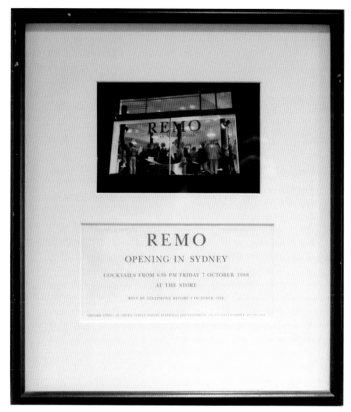

REMO opening night invitation and party, 7 October 1988

REMO
General Store

Ground floor interior
October 1993 catalogue

Printed Thing
Page 16

REMO catalogues

REMO 2.0
2007 home page

Customer network

Feature article in
HQ Magazine, 1991

1 2 3 4 5 6 7 8 9 10 11 12 13 14 15 16 17 18 19 20 21 22 23 24 25 26 27 28 29 30 31 32 33 34 35 36 37 38 39 40 41 42 43 44 45 46 47 48 49 50 51 52 53 54

1988 ◄──────► 1996

[26] Instinct & Intuition

Some things are really quite wonderful, but you can't always say why.

This is something that preoccupied me to an extreme degree when my livelihood as a merchant required this knowing without necessarily knowing why. I didn't always know why, however I was usually able to recognise the magic when I saw it ... at an instinctive and intuitive level.

Melanie and I used to play a game, and we still play it on occasion. It's called "the one thing" and it involves walking through an ostensibly daggy store and finding the one thing that is imbued with enough magic and special sauce to make it something that we might have included within the REMO General Store range in days gone by. It might be a single beeswax candle or a Chinese calendar or a wooden reel of red cotton or a referee's whistle. It's a fun game. You should try it.

The Fortune Teller Miracle Fish (a small red cellophane fish that is placed on outstretched palms to measure passion) was big on my list of magically appealing products, mostly because of the great graphics. So much so that I developed *a lot* of merchandise over the years bearing its image: T shirts, greeting cards, keyrings, badges ... even a specially woven Miracle Fish beach towel.

But maybe the hero in this poetic merchandise category was the Sea Shell Headphones, the product of my 1989 collaboration with the concept originators, Joyce Hinterding (artist) and Ian Hobbs (then a photographer). In all, the Sea Shell Headphones took me four dogged years of prototyping to bring to market as a shining star of the REMO General Store range. There are about 200 out there, confusing house cleaners all over the world.

Hands-free sound of the sea. What do you think?

The Sydney Morning Herald, 27 October 1988

Magic Added RemoGram, 1997

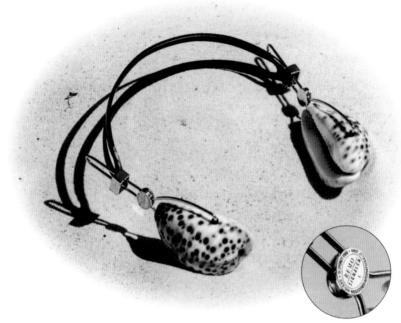

REMO Signalen Sea Shell Headphones, 1989

Fortune Teller
Miracle Fish

Cachou Lajaunie

8 Ball Keyring

Acme Thunderer

Chinese calendar

Ginger Candies

Mosquito Coil
design

Chickie

Fez design

Perkins Paste
T shirt

1 2 3 4 5 6 7 8 9 10 11 12 13 14 15 16 17 18 19 20 21 22 23 24 25 26 27 28 29 30 31 32 33 34 35 36 37 38 39 40 41 42 43 44 45 46 47 48 49 50 51 52 53 54

1989

[27] Systems & Creativity

Not everyone is the same in this respect, but for me, having a system in place enhances my capacity to be creative. It's like knowing that the bars of the jungle gym are solid and sturdy. When that's the case I feel able to swing more confidently ... and higher.

Also, when the creativity required is mostly about content, it becomes distracting to have to think about format. Others feel the same. I remember in the early days of *Colors* magazine, the Editor-in-Chief Tibor Kalman [47] used to make his collaborators crazy by changing the physical format of the magazine with each new issue. Once it settled into its standardised format, content providers were able to start focusing more on the generation of compelling editorial.

Here are five examples of where I have driven the development of a structure to support my own creative preference:

1. Crown Street Windows [44]. Designing for a constant environment with fixed dimensions.
2. Bondi Road Corner Posters [74]. Ditto.
3. REMO catalogues [43], After the big one in 1991, the format became simpler. Liberating.
4. My Uniform [87]. I would classify my uniform as a system that enhances my creativity.
5. TEDxSydney [75] program format has standardised at four sessions of 90 minutes each.

When I was merchandising for REMO in its most recent incarnation (2002 to 2012), I became quite fanatical about modularity, and the capacity to break the range down into uniform pods, either graphically as part of an image grid, or physically in the form of a perspex display system that I designed to enable us to create all sorts of configurations from the same basic units.

The final example is actually this book. Once I settled on the template for the spreads with my long-time layout designer Aivi Juske [84], it became much easier for me to start thinking about the words that I was going to write, and the images that I was going to use to accompany those words.

For some people this templated approach to creativity might be stifling, but for me it is both soothing and liberating.

REMO 100 poster concept, 2012

REMO merchandise pod
at euro caffe, 2003

Freestanding
pod doodle

Sample spread
1994 catalogue

Crown Street Window
October 1991

Bondi Road
Corner, 2009

1 2 3 4 5 6 7 8 9 10 11 12 13 14 15 16 17 18 19 20 21 22 23 24 25 26 27 28 29 30 31 32 33 34 35 36 37 38 39 40 41 42 43 44 45 46 47 48 49 50 51 52 53 54

1988   2012

[28] Photobooth Postcard

Many, many of our customers from the Darlinghurst REMO days had their photos taken in our old black and white photobooth. Kids had their growing up documented. Lovers had their love celebrated. And then there was a memorable year when my good friend Russell Cheek, whom I met when he was in The Castanet Club [17], took on the role of REMO Santa, thereby enabling him to don red acrylic garb and get up close and personal in a sweaty photobooth with hundreds of Christmas shoppers.

The photobooth also played a starring role in our 1989 Christmas card. That card, entitled "The Human Face of Retailing," was enclosed within a 16-page catalogue that we sent out to around 4,500 mailing list customers. (I can still recall the marathon in-store fold fest.)

The card in question spelt out the word "REMO" and involved lots of REMO people holding or using their favourite products. Two push pins, one red and one green, in place of the silver ones at the top of the card gave the requisite nod to the festive season. Pretty.

BUT ... the card represented much more than just that. For those who took the time to *think* about it, the image also communicated a collaborative spirit and a deep sense of fun. With less than a second between each vertical frame moving down each of the six strips, just think about what was involved in this exercise. Joyful mayhem.

People & Products

REMO Photobooth Postcard | The Human Face of Retailing, 1989

Our photobooth   Wall of honour   Photobooth postcard mayhem

1 2 3 4 5 6 7 8 9 10 11 12 13 14 15 16 17 18 19 20 21 22 23 24 25 26 27 28 29 30 31 32 33 34 35 36 37 38 39 40 41 42 43 44 45 46 47 48 49 50 51 52 53 54

1989

[29] Brand Soup

I have used this simple yet useful metaphor in my work with brands over the years.

Things that taste great are not always simple to make. Brands, like people, have personalities and flavours. Think of them as Brand Soup.

For REMO, the base of the soup was functionality and fitness for purpose, but into this was tossed unequal measures of: classicism, modernism, nostalgia, invention, technology, humour, wit, compassion, and so on …

The result was a tasty, yet quite complex, combination of flavours that went into making a (hopefully) delicious and unique whole.

But the cooking is never complete, and over time things need to be added … a sprinkle of this, a dash of that. The initial recipe is important, but the cooking even more so.

Also, the greater the number of ingredients, the harder it is for someone else to copy the flavour … even if they think they know the recipe.

This thinking all started as REMO soup, but, more recently, I've been working on TEDxSydney soup and General Thinking soup. People who get to taste these newer soups might detect some signature REMO flavours here and there. However, they are also different in significant ways.

What's your brand flavour? What are your ingredients?

TED Soup, 2012

REMO Soup, 1990

Functionality
(Fitness for purpose)

1 2 3 4 5 6 7 8 9 10 11 12 13 14 15 16 17 18 19 20 21 22 23 24 25 26 27 28 29 **30** 31 32 33 34 35 36 37 38 39 40 41 42 43 44 45 46 47 48 49 50 51 52 53 54

1990

[30] Product Development Vision

The most fun work thing that I've ever done has been to drive the development of my own eponymous REMO brand. (Once you taste that fruit, it's very hard to settle for less.)

Even before the adoption of the head graphic [39] as our logo, I had been mostly guided by my own needs and frustration. In 1989 I wrote this to customers:

*"We hold a strong vision for the ongoing development of products that address what we see to be a universal yearning for forgotten quality, purity and simplicity. **Not luxury**; rather – basic function peppered with some wit. Classic with a **twist** – timeless, friendly & trusted."*

I was also very sensitive about the relationship of the physical brand to the product. In the November 1991 customer newsletter I wrote this:

"It took a bit of playing around via fax machines with Michael Dupree and others before I was happy enough with this limerick to put it down in writing:– 'The product is the product, the product has a brand, but the brand is not the product.' (Catchy?) That's why you won't generally find our brand on the visible exterior of our products, but rather discreetly sewn inside. As proud as we are of the things we're willing to brand, we don't feel that the brand in itself should be obvious – the function of the item being more important than the identity of the sponsor."

In 1991 we adopted a modified version of Douglas Riccardi's phrenology head graphic as our "General Store" logo, and then it became even easier to figure out what we should be doing on various product development fronts. The graphic reminded us that our customers needed and desired certain things, and it lent itself to cross-category thinking, enabling the execution to be potentially much bigger than for a brand that is limited to a single category such as apparel.

And it all worked a treat. By 1994 a whopping 65% of our sales (and nearly 80% of our gross profits) were of REMO branded items. In decreasing order of volume that was represented by: clothing, homewares, T Shirt designs, stationery, food, skin/hair care, jewellery and miscellanea.

The flavour of the brand was the result of an intuitive and dynamic Brand Soup [29] "recipe" – a unique and delicate combination of ingredients: function, passion, classicism, intelligence, serendipity and wit.

REMO Brand Selection, 1995

REMO brand vision, 2011
Development driven by the REMO Logo [39]

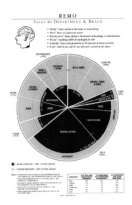

REMO brand by department
February 1993

1 2 3 4 5 6 7 8 9 10 11 12 13 14 15 16 17 18 19 20 21 22 23 24 25 26 27 28 29 30 31 32 33 34 35 36 37 38 39 40 41 42 43 44 45 46 47 48 49 50 51 52 53 54

1989   1993 1995   2011

[31] Eternity at REMO

This is such a Sydney story.

For the 37 years spanning 1930 to 1967, a man named Arthur Stace walked the streets of Sydney ... and wrote on them; one word, always the same word, in yellow chalk in large, elegant copperplate.

That word was "Eternity."

He worked before dawn, alone and in secret, travelling to a different neighbourhood every day. For decades this divine prank mystified the people of Sydney. The scrawls were an enigma. People grew up with them. Columnists wrote about them. Street sweepers swept around them. Artists like the late, great Martin Sharp were inspired by them.

Before his conversion to Christianity in 1930, Arthur was a derelict alcoholic on the "edge of insanity." Then one day at a Baptist Church he heard a noted give-em-Hell preacher shout to the congregation: *"I wish I could shout 'Eternity' through the streets of Sydney."* He repeated himself and kept shouting *"Eternity, Eternity."* The words rang in Arthur's head as he left the church. He began to cry, bent down and wrote it for the first time. He knew what he had to do.

Like many Sydneysiders of the right age, Martin Sharp recalls his first brush with Arthur Stace's Eternity. Indeed, Martin incorporated references to Arthur's Eternity in a number of works over the years.

I too remember coming across Arthur's Eternity chalkings from time to time in the Haymarket area of Sydney, and I recall the aura of mystery that was evoked.

So when I approached Martin with the idea in 1990, it wasn't hard to convince him that HE should be the one to create an Eternity design for REMO in tribute to Arthur Stace. The huge five-metre canvas adorned our Crown Street Window during November 1990 (jogging memories, triggering smiles, stopping traffic, even causing some accidents). Customer souvenirs for the homage included: limited edition prints, T Shirts, postcards, etc. I was never one to miss a good merchandising opportunity.

This was such a happy marriage for all concerned. Aside from Martin's mesmerising image, Eternity dovetailed perfectly with one of REMO's primary philosophies: the theme of anti-disposability *"Buy it once and own it forever."*, and our belief in the universal importance and value of commitment, perseverance and, most of all ... passion.

Eternity at REMO print, dedicated to Remo by Martin Sharp, 6 November 1990

Arthur Stace
"Mr Eternity"

With Martin Sharp
at REMO launch

Martin's
Eternity story

Martin painting the mural
Down to the wire

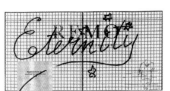

Martin's original scrawl
for our Crown Street Window

Eternity at
REMO

Martin in REMO boardroom
signing the prints

Eternity on the ground
floor at REMO, 1992

Sydney Harbour
Bridge, NYE 2000

At Martin's funeral
December 2013

1 2 3 4 5 6 7 8 9 10 11 12 13 14 15 16 17 18 19 20 21 22 23 24 25 26 27 28 29 30 31 32 33 34 35 36 37 38 39 40 41 42 43 44 45 46 47 48 49 50 51 52 53 54

1990

[32] I, Customer

Customer centricity, a central tenet of design thinking, is really no more than a marketplace reflection of the Golden Rule (otherwise known as the "ethic of reciprocity") that one should treat others as one would like others to treat oneself. (Some say that this is also what underpins all religious belief systems.)

For me the value of being driven by that empathy is all common sense, and it's that common sense that continues to underpin all of my thinking relating to brands and customer experiences.

Most RemoGrams begin with a stick figure, and quite often I'm thinking that the figure is me. What do *I* want this experience to be?

Similarly, the REMO head logo [39] represented our customers, but it was originally (and not accidentally) based on a photograph of my profile. As the development director for REMO branded merchandise [30] and the primary architect of the branded retail experience, I was mostly driven by my own self interest. What sort of shirts did *I* want to be able to buy, what kind of online experience did *I* want to have?

If enough people care about what *you* care about, you not only have a business, you can also take comfort in the knowledge that all you really need to do is please yourself.

PS: See Also The Community is the Brand [60] and THEM=US [47]

CUS ᵮ OMƎꓤ

You=Me [47]

Love, Work &
Money [7]

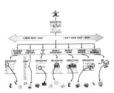

Paths to Merchandise
RemoGram, 1998

Cafés & Community [85]

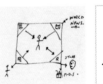

The REMO Logo [39]

1 2 3 4 5 6 7 8 9 10 11 12 13 14 15 16 17 18 19 20 21 22 23 24 25 26 27 28 29 30 31 32 33 34 35 36 37 38 39 40 41 42 43 44 45 46 47 48 49 50 51 52 53 54

1988

[33] Merchandise Iceberg

When the REMO General Store opened in Sydney in 1988, none of the original crew had all that much retailing experience. Being unconstrained by "conventional wisdom" enabled us to approach our merchandising mission from first principles.

I had always felt that we were in the *communications* business, and in order to drive that message home I often used the visual metaphor of the iceberg, where there is a lot more going on beneath the surface than above.

A traditional retail merchant will typically present merchandise as an end in and of itself: *"Here's a nice shiny pen. Do you like it? Do you want to buy it?"*

At REMO we always regarded the collection of molecules which made up the actual pen as just the tip of a large and very interesting contextual iceberg, thus:

"Paul Fisher spent a million dollars to achieve his objective of a writing instrument for NASA that would perform in the weightlessness of space ... Here are some customers that use the Fisher Space Pen, and here's what they think, etc., etc."

It's a different approach ... Bits v. Bytes. Traditional merchants sell molecules, but we told stories about products and the people/passion behind them, and sold souvenirs of those stories. (Those souvenirs just happen to have been made of molecules.) The REMO idea was never to sell per se, but rather to tell the STORIES that communicated the passion.

BRC #049, October 2011

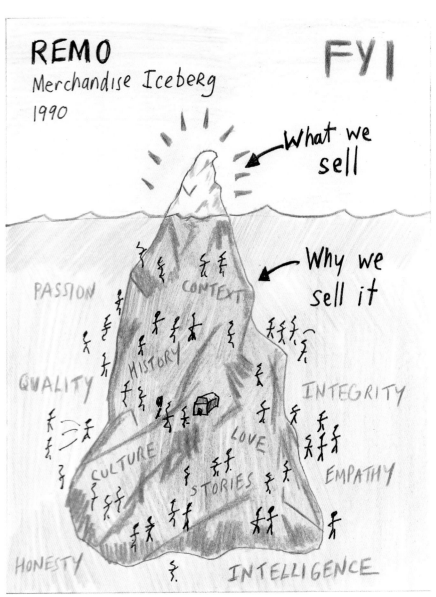

Bondi Road Corner Poster, October 2011

1 2 3 4 5 6 7 8 9 10 11 12 13 14 15 16 17 18 19 20 21 22 23 24 25 26 27 28 29 30 31 32 33 34 35 36 37 38 39 40 41 42 43 44 45 46 47 48 49 50 51 52 53 54

1990   2011

[34] My Island Thing

There's something about islands that really gets under my skin, in a good way, and my life is peppered with seminal or formative experiences that have happened on islands.

Here are five islands that have played a part in my life thus far:

1. **Salina,** the Æolian island in Sicily where my father was born [2]
2. **Australia,** the island continent that he relocated to in 1928 [61]
3. **Brecqhou,** the island that belonged to the charismatic Len Matchan [11]
4. **Wilson Island,** the island upon which I finalised my courtship of Melanie [38]
5. **Fire Island,** the island that I found so appealing when we were living in New York [59]

Also, when I'm dreaming big [40] I tend also to picture myself on a tiny and generic tropical island, either reclining on a chaise like a stick man from one of my doodles, or sitting at a table on a verandah with a pen in my hand and a clean note book in which to scribble.

The thing about small islands is that once explored, that's it. No further temptation of physical discovery to distract you from the task at hand, even if that task is complete relaxation.

The other thing about islands is that they exist outside the system and away from the mainstream. Even if you've read only a handful of the chapters in this book, you don't need to be Sigmund Freud to figure out why this would appeal to my personality.

30 JUNE 1991

Letter to Melanie [38]

Wilson Island [38]

Salina [2]

Australia [61]

Brecqhou [11]

Fire Island [59]

1 2 3 4 5 6 7 8 9 10 11 12 13 14 15 16 17 18 19 20 21 22 23 24 25 26 27 28 29 30 31 32 33 34 35 36 37 38 39 40 41 42 43 44 45 46 47 48 49 50 51 52 53 54

1960   1979   1991   2001

[35] Splayds

I've always thought that Splayds made a whole lot of sense.

A Splayd is a versatile combination of spoon, fork and knife in one (just think, it could have been "Splork") and it enables you to eat from a plate using one hand. It's an Australian invention dating back to the 40s, and a set of Splayds became the definitive wedding gift of the 70s.

Basically darling, you *"couldn't go wrong with a set of Splayds."*

Splayds were first made for a Sydney coffee shop called Martha Washington's, which became a popular spot for visiting US troops during World War II. Splayds became momentarily famous, and after the war were exported to the US to fill the demand fuelled by the servicemen returning home and spreading the word about this great new piece of flatware.

But, for whatever reason, the knowledge was lost. These days it's pretty hard to spot a Splayd outside of Australia and New Zealand.

Splayds were just about the most often rated and commented-on product available from both versions of the REMO General Store: 20th Century (offline) and 21st Century (online). Customers seemed to either really love or really hate the fact that we sold Splayds. This never bothered me. Early on I decided that making Splayds cool [3] was going to be one of my life's great achievements. I had the patience, and if I could do it for Splayds, I could do it for anything.

I'm not sure that I ever succeeded … although we did sell thousands of Splayd sets over the years. It concerns me sometimes that I can't find any at home. I have my suspicions, as I don't think that I was ever able to convert Melanie over to my way of thinking.

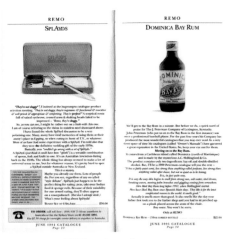

REMO catalogue, June 1991

1 2 3 4 5 6 7 8 9 10 11 12 13 14 15 16 17 18 19 20 21 22 23 24 25 26 27 28 29 30 31 32 33 34 35 36 37 38 39 40 41 42 43 44 45 46 47 48 49 50 51 52 53 54

1991

[36] Stripey Things & Tempus Fugit

Two products from the REMO branded archive are worthy of special mention: the classic REMO Stripey Thing and the Tempus Fugit Wallplanner. Along with the REMO T shirt, these two things became iconic and emblematic of the REMO General Store range.

The perennial appeal of Stripey Things is not that surprising. I'd become of aware of their timeless appeal before I'd even thought of making the REMO version, and in fact before I'd even thought of launching REMO itself. I was living in New York and my girl friend Heather Martin was from Maine. We tried to buy her a stripey from LL Bean and were told that they were out of stock. Such was our horror that we wrote to them, and they wrote back, equally horrified and repentant. The item had been in continuous production since 1967 and was a regular big seller. (I filed that bit of information away in the back of my head somewhere.)

Our version was similar but different. The designer Katerina Skvorc and I obsessed over that stripe ratio for a long while, eventually settling on 1 to 1.5. I still use this visual characteristic to identify a REMO Stripey from a distance; and here in Sydney there are still *lots* of them out there, which is not remarkable, in that we sold many tens of thousands of them over the years. Other than T shirts it was our single biggest seller, and although we haven't sold them for many years I still receive a weekly email from an orphaned customer in desperate need of a Stripey Thing.

This from the Lovemarks [66] website:

Love is ...
"REMO is the antithesis of blah, an online Aladdin's cave, the essence of must have and always, but always.....fun. It's a reminder of a misspent youth, the excitement of providing the perfect gift and knowing that the recipient will not be able to resist REMO-ing in return. Love is a REMO Stripey Thing."
Marcia, Australia – 19 November 2003

We developed our first *Tempus Fugit* wallplanner for our own internal organisational needs back in 1991. We marketed an A1 sized version that year that was an immediate and big hit. A wallplanner is a magical organisational tool. It is strangely soothing to get all of your special events and deadlines up there on the wall and visible in a single view. And crossing out the boxes becomes a regular daily treat. Other wallplanners exist of course, but they are either very bland or very ugly. Ours was cool and gorgeously graphic.

And the point is?

Merchandise that is timeless and useful will always win in the long run, and some things are so universally appealing that they transcend the Zeitgeist.

Katerina tests stripe width
ratio on Hugh Ramage

General Thinker ⸙ remogiuffre.com/stripeyfugit

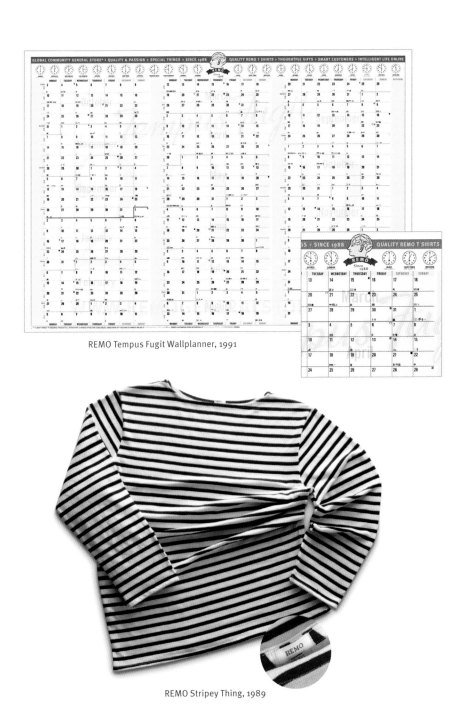

REMO Tempus Fugit Wallplanner, 1991

REMO Stripey Thing, 1989

1 2 3 4 5 6 7 8 9 10 11 12 13 14 15 16 17 18 19 20 21 22 23 24 25 26 27 28 29 30 31 32 33 34 35 36 37 38 39 40 41 42 43 44 45 46 47 48 49 50 51 52 53 54

1989 1991

[37] Special Places

My primary focus as a merchant was on the curation and development of a unique portfolio of "Special Things;" but, in addition to this, I have always been fascinated by the notion of "Special Places."

In the very early REMO [25] days we would sometimes celebrate special places with T shirt designs. Examples of this would have included: 10th Street Baths (celebrating the Russian & Turkish Baths that I would frequent when living in New York as a student), Bondi Icebergs (celebrating my favourite local place), ISO (a Keith Haring design developed for the sushi restaurant in the East Village that we both patronised in the 80s), and Florent (a more recent design that paid homage to an iconic diner in the meatpacking district of New York that became the focus for much activism and creativity in the 90s).

Special Places became a feature of the online REMO 2.0 experience; although, in that case, it was less about my opinions and more about harnessing the collective knowledge and intelligence of the customer community. Customers would nominate special places and other customers were able to comment on those choices. It actually became quite useful for me personally as a source of advice for places to frequent while travelling.

So, what makes a place special?

The answer is not straightforward. There's some black magic and instinct [26] involved. You feel it when you see it, like the first time I visited the Oyster Bar at Grand Central Station in New York. For me personally, authenticity is critical. The Odeon restaurant in TriBeCa had it, but a restaurant in the meatpacking district by the same owner Keith McNally – called Pastis and mocked up to look like a Parisian café – did not.

The original REMO Store in Darlinghurst was, for me and others, a quintessentially special place. So, I know first hand that the experience architecture required for the establishment of a special place can be complicated … even for simple places.

Here's to the people who are able to pull it off.

REMO 10th Street Baths T shirt design, 1989

REMO Oxford Street
window, 1988

Remo with Florent
at Florent

The Oyster Bar
Grand Central Station

Odeon Restaurant
in TriBeCa

Sean's at
Bondi Beach

Bondi Icebergs [88]

Sydney Opera House
See TEDxSydney [75]

Adelaide Central
Market

Icebergs Dining
Room and Bar

Alex Kalman at
Mmuseumm in NYC

1 2 3 4 5 6 7 8 9 10 11 12 13 14 15 16 17 18 19 20 21 22 23 24 25 26 27 28 29 30 31 32 33 34 35 36 37 38 39 40 41 42 43 44 45 46 47 48 49 50 51 52 53 54

1991

[38] Courting Melanie Dames

The defining relationship of my life is the one I've shared with Melanie, my wife and the mother of our two children. It's a relationship that exists and thrives due largely to my two biggest strengths: clarity of vision and persistence beyond reason.

We met in late 1987 at a restaurant in Bondi. I was back in Sydney from New York and she was freshly returned from her five years of life in Paris. If it wasn't love at first sight, it was pretty damn close. I quickly became obsessed as we became friends. It blossomed on 25 April 1988 on my 28th birthday. Melanie had agreed to host a party at her place in Potts Point. I ended up staying the night. I was well and truly smitten.

For me that night was the beginning of the rest of my life. For her it had been a pleasant but somewhat regrettable one night stand with a friend. I spent the next three years trying to convince her otherwise, and she spent the same three years steadfastly uninterested.

Her indifference to me at that level over those years is legend. I was a big letter writer, and I wrote to her a lot. I also sent her faxes from various cities when on buying trips for REMO [25], keeping her up to date with my "fascinating" life, a life that I was desperate for her to share. I'm told that she would position the fax machine directly over the waste paper bin, and into that bin would tumble my densely crafted missives. Quite an image.

We both had other relationships during those three years, but I kept returning to an imagined life with Melanie. It was something that I couldn't see beyond. Very few people in Sydney knew of this obsession. It was my most painful secret.

Come 1991, and just like the Amy Irving character's feelings for the pickle guy in *Crossing Delancey*, or Billy Crystal and Meg Ryan in *When Harry Met Sally* ... something finally started to change between Melanie and me. The three-year drought broke on a Sunday in mid-June. I had accompanied Melanie to a lunch in Whale Beach. She was driving and we were listening to the *Popeye* soundtrack. We both felt the same sense of euphoria. I ended up staying the night at her place in Point Piper. (It had been a long time between drinks.)

But my work was not done. Over the next week or two I peppered her with notes and letters, using every *carpe diem* metaphor that I was able to muster. The requirement in life to take the momentary risk of *"stepping off the jetty"* and *"losing sight of the shore"* in order to discover truth and happiness were recurrent and suitably nautical themes.

In a 21 June letter I wrote with confidence and presumption:

"You will accompany me on these journeys Melanie ... I can feel it in my bones. I can see it & I can touch it ... You can see it too. (Indeed I can sometimes see you seeing it.) You will in fact come to my conclusion, but you will have to do so on your own. This might take days, weeks or even months. It won't take years. Actually, I think it's all happening right now – a lot faster than you might have thought it would. The reactor is in meltdown. This may be confusing."

But there was one more letter to come ... and oh what a letter. I wrote it on Wilson Island [34] as a last ditch attempt to shock and awe her with my clarity and commitment; 43 handwritten pages interweaving self-reflection with biography, family history and future dreams. It was the most important thing I'd ever written, and I didn't leave anything out.

General Thinker ⨍ remogiuffre.com/courtingmelanie

FOR Melanie

30 JUNE 1991

Letter to Melanie from Wilson Island

Melanie

21 June Letter

Wilson Island [34]

On our wedding day, 24 November 1991

I hand-delivered the letter on Sunday 30 June. When I called from the airport she seemed a bit annoyed, but reluctantly agreed to see me. As Melanie tells the story, the *instant* she saw me standing there in the doorway with my bag and letter all resistance finally crumbled and she *knew* that we would indeed be together for the rest of our lives. The *mere fact* of that letter had meant more that the specifics of its content. We got engaged that very night, totally blindsiding our friends and families, and were married within months.

[39] The REMO Logo

This is the REMO logo ... eerily familiar to many of you I'm sure.

It was designed to represent US as well as representing YOU. #

It was adopted to remind us that we all need and desire certain things in life: quality foods, clothing, stationery, homewares, skincare, jewellery, other personal items and unique gifts. We also need to be informed, amused, entertained and loved.

The head device used to drive everything we did in our quest to serve and delight customers.

And what of its design origin?

In 1989 New York-based designer Douglas Riccardi (then working at the M&Co. Design Group) developed a T shirt design for us based on a Polaroid of the profile of me ... taken during one of my many pilgrimages to the M&Co. offices in Manhattan to meet with Tibor Kalman [47].

The original phrenology-head-inspired T Shirt design was silk screened in black with the Seven Deadly Sins printed on one side and the Seven Heavenly Virtues printed on the other. Then in 1991 we had the idea to replace the sins and virtues with these new REMO departmental words to create an enduring symbol for our General Store. In 1999 we added a blue REMO ribbon that also conveniently served to conceal the severed neck.

This *"do unto others"* realisation and recognition that we are first and foremost our own customers is a recurrent theme in my work and thinking. See also: [30], [32], [56] and [60]

Douglas Riccardi ...

shoots Remo's profile
at M&Co. in New York

Seven Deadly Sins
1989

General Store head
1991

Final logo with
ribbon, 1999

1 2 3 4 5 6 7 8 9 10 11 12 13 14 15 16 17 18 19 20 21 22 23 24 25 26 27 28 29 30 31 32 33 34 35 36 37 38 39 40 41 42 43 44 45 46 47 48 49 50 51 52 53 54

1989 1991   1999

[40] Dreaming Big

I initially regarded REMO General Store as a lifestyle choice, choosing to live a life of passion, even if that life was going to be a relatively small life. It was only after REMO got going that my eyes were opened to the fact that it actually had the potential to go global and get big. *Who'd 'a thunk it?*

I've never had a problem thinking big. I'm good at surveying the landscape from a height of 50,000 feet. I'm also very good with the details. I can clearly see the leaves on all of the trees, and I notice when one is out of place. Where I'm not as good is with the mid-range stuff, in other words making sure that all of the trees bearing those leaves are doing what they need to be doing in order to support the development of that landscape.

The response to our award-winning November 1991 catalogue [43] had been remarkable, and smart people all over the world were beginning to tell me that this brand had universal appeal and could go all the way. My obsession, as a big picture guy, was trying to work out the best global rollout model for REMO. I did my marketplace homework: mecca plus stores (Tiffany & Co.), multi-landmark (Hard Rock Cafe), multi-boutique (Chanel), mail order only (LL Bean), and so on ...

The model I chose for REMO at the time is illustrated by this RemoGram penned while on holiday in Fiji in late 1992. There are a few landmark General Stores in there, but all of those little ® things are something else *"REMO Café / Bar / Media Depot / General Store Trading Posts."* The whole thing was supported by: an annual catalogue/almanac/ magazine (which came with a CD ROM version, remember those?), and zoned smaller format *"seasonal/promotional catalogues."* The network also included some other branded experiences e.g. weekenders, spas, etc. There were even a few branded little island resorts, places where our customers could get away from it all and relax. (There's a little stick guy reclining on a lounge on one of those islands. I have a feeling that I was imagining myself in that situation when I included him.)

Of course, this was SO FAR AWAY from the reality of the situation at the time as to be ludicrous. The reality of REMO was closer to a poorly managed and chronically under-capitalised small business.

The business failures I've experienced on the REMO front have made me more conscious of this paradox of dreaming big while surviving small. Dreaming big is not something that I've stopped doing, this audacity of hope being a core part of my DNA [1]. However, now I'm more focused on working with people who are better than I am at looking after those trees.

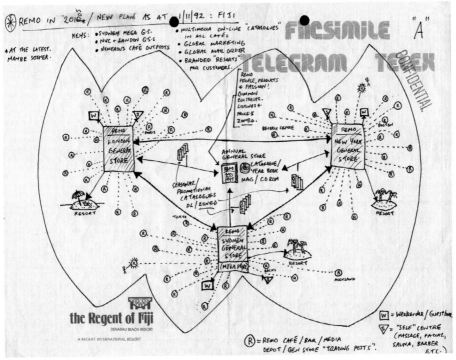

REMO global network envisioning, 1992

Columbia Business School
1984 to 1986

The Thinker(s)
1985

Rollout models
1992

Head in Clouds
design, 1996

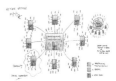

Retail rollout vision
2011

1 2 3 4 5 6 7 8 9 10 11 12 13 14 15 16 17 18 19 20 21 22 23 24 25 26 27 28 29 30 31 32 33 34 35 36 37 38 39 40 41 42 43 44 45 46 47 48 49 50 51 52 53 54

1992

[41] People, Quality & Passion

The real power of the REMO General Store [25] lay in the way it approached its merchandising. Traditional merchants sell products; but we told stories about products and the people/passion behind them. The products became souvenirs of those stories.

Indeed, at the end of the day literally everything boils down to individual people; and behind every single product we presented on our shelves was a person and his or her passion. And passion was a major thread linking the wildly diverse range of merchandise that we presented via the REMO store and catalogues: passion for the soap produced, passion for the watch designed, the fabric sourced, the coffee roasted, the magazine published ... passion, commitment and enthusiasm.

By way of example, I was personally inspired by the passion that:

+ Guglielmo "Gughi" Valobra had for his Genovese Valobra Soaps
+ Retired Vermont Senator Roger Eddy had for his kitchen-table made Audubon Bird Calls
+ New York designer Tibor Kalman had for his range of M&Co. watches
+ Keith Haring had for his Pop Shop merchandise (which I represented in Australia)
+ The Morse family had for their Kiehl's Pharmacy range of skincare products
+ Wanny di Filippo had for his Il Bisonte brand of leather bags and accessories
+ Sydney artist Martin Sharp had for Arthur Stace and his Eternity message

In all these instances I enjoyed a direct and personal relationship with the people, thereby becoming the conduit of that passion back to the REMO customer network. The fact that I would more often than not have this direct relationship with the merchandise originator imbued our range with more meaning and relevance that it would have otherwise enjoyed. That made it feel all the more authentic. We weren't just selling anonymous stuff sourced from a trade show [78]. We were providing a platform for some really impressive people to tell us their passionate merchandise stories.

Real people. Real passion. Real products.

Richard Glover shoots us
for the back cover, 1990

Back cover of the REMO catalogue, 1990

With "Gughi" Valobra
Valobra Soaps

Audubon Bird Call
by Roger Eddy

With Tibor and
Maira Kalman, 1991

Keith Haring
Pop Shop

With Aaron Morse
Kiehl's Pharmacy

LOVE Sign by Al
James, 2004

With Wanny di Filippo
Il Bisonte Leather

Martin Sharp at home with
Eternity swimming cap

REMO Head [39]
love segment

1 2 3 4 5 6 7 8 9 10 11 12 13 14 15 16 17 18 19 20 21 22 23 24 25 26 27 28 29 30 31 32 33 34 35 36 37 38 39 40 41 42 43 44 45 46 47 48 49 50 51 52 53 54

1988 ◄────► 1996   2002 ◄────► 2012

[42] Barrow Man

The REMO General Store was locally famous for its Crown Street Windows [44]. Our corner was exposed to an enormous amount of traffic, both people and cars, and we changed the display every couple of weeks. It's how we spoke to the City of Sydney and its citizens.

The displays were not always commercial, and this window display in tribute to Sydney's Barrow Man has an interesting back story.

Joseph Cindric (a post-war immigrant from Yugoslavia for whom things did *not* go well) was a man who pushed a handmade trolley around the Sydney CBD for decades. From the 60s to the 80s he was very much a part of those parts of the city where he often trudged or slept during the day. He wore a dirty white helmet and a fixed, stony gaze.

Until Cindric's death, almost no one knew his name. Even Richard Goodwin, the noted Australian artist/architect whose sculptural career was partly inspired by the trolley man, and who filmed and photographed him for years, did not know until one day in 1994 when a nursing home rang him with the news of Cindric's death. *"Who is Joseph Cindric?"* Goodwin replied, before agreeing to be one of the few mourners at Cindric's funeral.

I was seated next to Richard at a charity dinner soon after that funeral. He told me his Barrow Man story, and I remarked on its similarity to the Eternity story [31]. We both expressed regret and some sadness that Joseph's passing had gone unnoticed, and later that night I resolved to do something about it.

Richard had left me with a doodle on a napkin. I commissioned our signwriter to make a model from that doodle for our Crown Street Window. And so, Joseph appeared with his trolley and on the street, one last time for the people of Sydney ... and we were all given the chance to pay our last respects to one hard life lived.

We received a significant amount of positive feedback for that window display, and, although this wasn't the motivation, it served to further enhance the crazy levels of loyalty that customers had for REMO in those Darlinghurst days.

Good karma is good for business.

PS: Joseph's trolley, the model made for the window display and the original napkin bearing Richard's doodle are all now part of the collection at Sydney's Powerhouse Museum.

Barrow Man at REMO, 1994

REMO Crown Street Window, September 1994

Barrow Man

Richard Goodwin

Richard's napkin sketch

Powerhouse Museum, Sydney

1 2 3 4 5 6 7 8 9 10 11 12 13 14 15 16 17 18 19 20 21 22 23 24 25 26 27 28 29 30 31 32 33 34 35 36 37 38 39 40 41 42 43 44 45 46 47 48 49 50 51 52 53 54

1994

[43] Being the Best

For much of my working life I have been a retail "merchant" amidst a sea of peers doing other more popular, contemporary or "normal" things: artists, designers, lawyers, bankers, and so on … The good thing about being on a niche career path is that you actually have a shot at being the best, and by "best" I mean best in the world.

Q: Was the physical REMO General Store a world-beating experience?
A: Maybe. In fact I would say probably. It was quite a remarkable place.

REMO catalogues, however, achieved at a whole other level, and I have no doubt that for a period of time we were setting the standard worldwide, influencing all sorts of brands and people. Our November 1991 Catalogue (dated 1992 on the cover) won Australian *Catalogue of the Year* … and ended up attracting global attention. Apart from anything else, it's the whole reason I got involved with TED [45].

Anyway, please allow me to boast a little by including a few quotes from the archive:

"It was probably inevitable that REMO won. Any person who has one of the REMO catalogues won't even lend it to you. The one that was first submitted to the ACA office vanished. The judges couldn't stop reading it. You had to pry it away from them."
Stuart Gibb-Cumming, Chairman of Judges, Australian Catalogue Awards (1991)

"He's got the best store in the world. By far. His are ventures that screw up preconceived notions about what a store should be, or what a catalog should be. They are being watched very carefully by all the retail and catalog giants around the world. His reputation precedes him. People are very much aware of him here in New York. I mean, big people are very much aware of what he's doing. A New York REMO would blow everyone out of the water."
Tibor Kalman, New York Designer, Quoted in Australian *HQ* magazine (1991)

"Truly the Best, No. 1: REMO. No ball game here. Even though I'm a US chauvinist, top honours go to an Australian catalog that many Americans have never had the exhilarating pleasure of seeing. REMO's copy makes all other catalogs seem amateurish. It's so good, it's a cover-to-cover "read." REMO is so good, in fact, it's hard to describe. I have never before encountered a catalog in which the blend of marketing and wordsmith mastery has been so perfect."
Herschell Gordon-Lewis, "The best and the worst of 1992" US *Catalog Age* (1993)

Shucks

So maybe that November 1991 "Mother of All Catalogues" (that's what we were calling it at the time) *was* worth all of the pain? I would say … definitely.

Lesson?

Really hard work pays off, and if you literally want to be the BEST at something, it helps to be somewhat of an outlier doing something that not too many other smart people are doing.

1991
CATALOGUE OF THE YEAR
AUSTRALIAN CATALOGUE AWARDS
Melbourne – February 1992

REMO

AUSTRALIA $5.00

92

REMO

1992

The Mother of All REMO Catalogues, November 1991 for 1992

Remo the
Merchant

REMO catalogues

US *Catalog
Age*, 1993

Welcome praise from Tibor

John Peterman
The J. Peterman Company

1 2 3 4 5 6 7 8 9 10 11 12 13 14 15 16 17 18 19 20 21 22 23 24 25 26 27 28 29 30 31 32 33 34 35 36 37 38 39 40 41 42 43 44 45 46 47 48 49 50 51 52 53 54

1989 ◀——▶ 1995

[44] Crown Street Windows

The original REMO General Store was located in a gracious old Victorian building located at the corner of Crown and Oxford Streets in Sydney's Darlinghurst. There was a window display on Oxford Street in which we would typically feature merchandise. That was for the benefit of the people on foot.

The main game, however, was a five-metre-long window on Crown Street: highly visible to people walking east up Oxford Street; but, more importantly, to the drivers and passengers of the endless stream of cars and buses making their way along Oxford Street. And also down the one-way Crown Street, heading north via the Sydney Harbour Bridge.

Put simply, this was an extraordinarily visible corner, and I was determined to use the exposure to the maximum degree possible. From early on my various design collaborators and I decided to take a very broad brush and graphic approach to the window displays. Phillip Parr, the sign writer I was working with, became skilled at the transformation of my ideas scrawled onto napkins and bits of paper into bright gleaming installations.

On the facing page are a selection of Crown Street Windows from the years 1988 to 1994.

Some of them were kinetic. The green Ho, Ho, Ho's from Christmas 1989 rollicked up and down against a red background. The giant gold fob watch from December 1993 swung back and forth against a spiraling red and green background with frosted lettering on the glass that suggested to the duly hypnotised that they buy all of their gifts at REMO. The most memorable window happened in November 1990 when we installed an original Martin Sharp Eternity [31] mural, in memory of "Mr Eternity" Arthur Stace.

People were very fond of our Crown Street Windows, and they became an iconic addition to the culture and streetscape of Sydney. So much so (and even *I* find it hard to believe this in retrospect), I was actually able to convince Telecom, the then Government-owned telecommunications provider, to move a phone box a few metres down the hill so that the visual frame of the window could be uninterrupted for the people and cars travelling up Oxford Street. (I would love to have seen the justification given for that work order.)

The window installations were also a very effective use of scarce marketing resources. The actual displays didn't cost that much (typically a couple of hundred dollars), and so we could change them every two or three weeks. The biggest cost was the creative one, as the pressure was always on to come up with something visually appealing and worthy enough for all of our smart customers [58].

REMO Crown Street Windows
1988 to 1996

Valentine's Day (spinning heart)
February 1991

HO, HO, HO (moving up and down)
December 1989

Scrabble REMO
October 1991

Cheers Anyway (during recession)
December 1990

LOVED
February 1992

The Castanet Club Movie [17]
April 1991

Worldwide Mail Order Service
June 1991

Don't Forget Fathers Day
September 1991

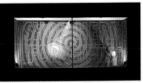

Shop Here for Gifts (swinging watch)
December 1993

Arthur Stace's Eternity [31]
March 1991

Barrow Man Tribute [42]
September 1994

Santa's Christmas Countdown
December 1994

Fortune Cookie Christmas
December 1992

Evolution of a CustOMER [58]
May 1992

REMO Cornucopia
October 1992

Japanese Apple
January 1993

Smiling REMO People [52]
October 1995

Au Revoir GOOD BUY [51]
April 1996

[45] My TED Story

The November 1991 REMO catalogue [43] attracted a lot of international attention to what I was doing in Sydney. Somehow – maybe he was on our mailing list – Richard Saul Wurman, the founder of TED, got to see one. He liked it a lot. So much so that he sent me a fax (no email in those days) inviting me to the next TED conference as his guest, on the condition that I came with enough of those catalogues to include in all of the "TEDster" gift bags. Given that RSW was the originator of the term "information architect," this was an extra flattering ask. If anyone's design opinion mattered to me at that time, it was his.

For me this was a win win. Not only was I being asked to attend what sounded, even in those very early days, to be a pretty cool event for free; I was being invited to actually market my wares to all of the interesting and insanely high-powered attendees. A great opportunity for a show off like me.

So I attended TED4 in Kobe, Japan in 1993, and then in Monterey for the next few years. After a multi-year-going-broke hiatus (ironically I was living much closer to the Monterey conference home in the US for much of this time) I started re-attending the not for profit Chris Anderson version, and have managed to return just about every year since then.

In the REMO days my attendance at TED was always something of a paradox, and the cause of some family tension. For 95% of the year I had my head down and my tail up working on the endless details and chronic cash flow issues being faced by my small Sydney-based business, but for one precious week I got to convene and make friends with people operating at the very tip of the world's new economy pyramid. (Too many names to drop.)

But there was a business connection too. For many years REMO was the official supplier of T shirts to TED; and that's how many TEDsters know me to this day, as the "T Shirt Guy" [46]. Very few of the old guard attendees would not have at least one REMO T shirt sitting in the wardrobe, if only for use at bed time.

Over the years I've worked on lots of other fun projects with TED: many different T shirt designs, early TED.com thinking and my ongoing work as licensee for TEDxSydney [75].

But, back to the community. The men and women that I'm privileged to spend time with each year at TED are people who have, in some cases, known me for over 20 years. That's a lot of history. It's the *tribe* that I'm attracted to, even more than the content (so effectively manifested by TED Talks). For me, the people always come first.

| With Stefan Sagmeister | With Karen Wickre | With Seth Godin |
| TED 2014 | TED 2008 | TED 2008 |

Chris Anderson and Tom Rielly draw the REMO General Store stage prize at TED 2008

Richard Saul
Wurman

Gift for TED4 Kobe
attendees

REMO for TED
T shirt design

Pitched vision for
TED.com, 1997

With REMO Printed
Thing at TED, 2008

With Tom Rielly my good
TEDster friend since 1993

REMO for TED
product ideas, 2008

TED 2010
T shirt

Guest curator
TED 2011

With Chris
Anderson, 2012

1 2 3 4 5 6 7 8 9 10 11 12 13 14 15 16 17 18 19 20 21 22 23 24 25 26 27 28 29 30 31 32 33 34 35 36 37 38 39 40 41 42 43 44 45 46 47 48 49 50 51 52 53 54

1993 ◄———— ————► 2014

[46] The T Shirt Guy

For a communicating guy [20] who is interested in design, a T shirt business is really a perfect thing. I guess I intuitively figured this out early on, and well before the days of REMO T shirts [46], because my past is littered with T shirt designs.

In 1983 while at The College of Law I designed a T shirt in celebration of my Quentin Steele [15] character, and the other members of "Club Delta." Wayne Golding, working with Dare Jennings at MAMBO, would print them for me in his spare bedroom in Redfern.

In 1984 I became the T Shirt guy at Baker & McKenzie [16], and if people really wanted to do some serious client schmoozing, they would commission me to design one off tees that my friend Mark Stanford would use an airbrush to make.

By 1985, in tandem with my full time studies at Columbia Business School, I was designing and selling silk-screened T Shirts in the East Village. That was the year I created my own iconic Take Out Coffee Cup [22] design for Design East ... along with Fish Head [21] and Rubber Chicken.

So, when I got around to REMO General Store [25] in 1988, it made sense that the first ever product developed from scratch bearing the REMO brand would be an exclusive range of designs on very high quality 100% cotton T shirts. For the launch I engaged with a global network of designers. Even by then I knew a bunch of good ones. Each was commissioned to create a design for the store and was paid royalties on sales.

REMO positioned the T shirt not so much as an item of apparel, but as a platform for ideas and a canvas. Indeed, that's how they were displayed, within frames on the wall.

Over the years we created, commissioned and marketed hundreds of unique designs, and we sold hundreds of thousands. The REMO T shirt became a design icon, not just in Australia but, within certain circles, all over the world.

Much of the international profile for the REMO T shirt was due to my role as the T Shirt Guy for the TED Conferences [45]. Over the years I designed many versions for speakers, VIPs and ultimately the attendees themselves. All of those T Shirts ended up in very good homes.

One of the reasons I took on TEDxSydney [75] was to bring home the message that I was more than just the T Shirt Guy. I think I've managed to do that. Even so, sometimes I feel a gentle tug in that direction; and if I do something with the REMO brand ever again, I feel sure that it will involve T shirts in some way.

With Tiny Tim at the REMO
T shirt wall in 1991

Preparing to send REMO T shirts for TED 2008 to Monterey and Aspen

Wayne Golding prints
Club Delta T shirts, 1983

Rubber Chicken
1985

Design East
display, 1986

T shirt ad for
PAPER, 1985

REMO Organic
Australian, 2011

Designs spread for 2008 Printed Thing [72]

1 2 3 4 5 6 7 8 9 10 11 12 13 14 15 16 17 18 19 20 21 22 23 24 25 26 27 28 29 30 31 32 33 34 35 36 37 38 39 40 41 42 43 44 45 46 47 48 49 50 51 52 53 54

1988 ← → 1996   2002 ← → 2012

[47] THEM=US

The THEM=US design was initially manifest as an enamel lapel pin in 1992 by the New York based M&Co. design group. The message was originally a reference to Ronald Reagan's non-response to the AIDS epidemic and an attempted eradication of the perceived wall between the ill and the healthy.

Tibor Kalman (1949 to 1999), the inspired leader of M&Co., was a big creative influence for me.

We met in New York in 1987. I had noticed that all of the ads that I liked in PAPER magazine (e.g. for Restaurant Florent and the designer Denise Carbonel) had been designed by M&Co. designers, and although I was still more than a year away from having any good reason to do so, on a hunch, I went to visit Tibor and kicked off our relationship.

We became collaborators and friends, and when I launched REMO in 1988 I included within our range all the items designed by M&Co. Labs e.g. their witty range of watches.

However, back to THEM=US.

I always thought that the message was bigger than the original application, and could in fact apply to any traditionally polarised situation:

+ Poor = Rich   + Palestinian = Israeli
+ Black = White   + Refugee = Resident
+ Gay = Straight   + Polluter = Polluted

It's really just a restatement of the Golden Rule – an "ethic of reciprocity" that dates back to antiquity. Basically it involves a person having empathy with others [32].

As an aside, I also adopted this idea in the context of an online business model [56] when, in 1999, and in an attempt to articulate the notion of customer-driven commerce to Silicon Valley VCs, I coined the phrase "B=C" to describe my particular REMO General Store [25] take on the traditional "B to C" retailing model.

Finally, and most recently, we included a THEM=US badge in all of the bags for the attendees of TEDxSydney 2014 [75]. Our lunch that day had been prepared from ingredients grown or baked by refugees or asylum seekers, and I wanted to remind people about the context and spirit with which we should be debating the treatment of people seeking refuge or asylum in Australia.

BRC #050, October 2011

General Thinker ⨍ remogiuffre.com/themus

REMO Bondi Road Corner Poster, October 2011

M&Co. enamel pin
1992

Tibor Kalman
1949 to 1999

With the Ubaldi brothers
at euro caffe, 2003

THEM=US T shirt in
the wild, 2011

Attendee Button
TEDxSydney 2014

1 2 3 4 5 6 7 8 9 10 11 12 13 14 15 16 17 18 19 20 21 22 23 24 25 26 27 28 29 30 31 32 33 34 35 36 37 38 39 40 41 42 43 44 45 46 47 48 49 50 51 52 53 54

1992   2011

[48] Context & Purpose

It's always better when people understand *why* they are doing what they are doing, and ideally why those reasons are *worthwhile*. Being able to give people context and a shared sense of purpose is an important part of being an effective leader.

In the October 1995 REMO catalogue [43] under the heading "Our Mission" I wrote:

"What's it all about? Why do we do what we do? What's the point?

*"Our **Mission** is to establish, serve and continually **delight** an **international community** of **happy** & **passionate** Customers, Staff & Friends. In the pursuit of this "Mission" we try our hardest to continually observe and apply the following **Core Values**:"*

Then, after listing 10 different core values and organisational drivers, I finish with:

*"And **you** just thought we sold you stuff."*

Similarly, in relation to my more recent work with TEDxSydney [75], I posed this question in a pre-meeting memo to the organising team:

"As many of you would know, I'm big on the articulation of organisational purpose ... and for that purpose to be something that people feel is worthwhile. It puts everything else into context. So, given that [working on TEDxSydney] is not a money earner of significance for any of us, why do we do what we do, both organisationally and indeed personally?"

Finally, even if it's not yet clear what the purpose of something is, I like to have the topic addressed. In the About section of the General Thinking [63] website I write:

*"The primary raison d'être for the General Thinking Network is simply to **BE** ... a networking platform and a source of support, inspiration and opportunity for its own members. Over and above this, what it **DOES** will become apparent over time; the network being responsible for its own development."*

If people understand the nature of the journey they are taking, they are more likely to feel good about coming along for the ride. The key here is honest communication.

People don't like being treated as cogs in a machine, soldiers just taking orders. Even the most menial task becomes noble if it can be appreciated as part of a bigger picture.

PEOPLE, QUALITY & PASSION

Where it all began: Oxford Street at Crown Street – 1988

OUR MISSION

What's it all about? Why do we do what we do? What's the point?

Our **MISSION** is to establish, serve and continually **delight** an **international community** of **happy & passionate** Customers, Staff & Friends.

In the pursuit of this "MISSION" we try our hardest to consistently observe and apply the following **CORE VALUES**:

- **Quality** in all we create and all we do – *"Buy it once and own it forever."*
- **Innovation & Creativity** – *"Imagination is more important than knowledge."*
- **Intelligence & Common Sense** – See "SMART CUSTOMERS" on p. 62
- **Functionalism** – *"To decide not to design is to design."* (See Opposite)
- **Passion, Commitment & Enthusiasm** – *"See the ball … move to the ball."*
- **Integrity, Friendliness, Openness (& Humour)** – *"Honesty is the best policy."*
- **Teamwork** and **Individuality** – *"The Power of One + One + One … "*
- **Magic, Wonderment & Serendipity** – *"Trust your Instinct"*
- **Tolerance & Support** for those less fortunate – *"Them=Us"*
- **Growth & Profitability** – *"Build the business, grow the Brand, spread the word."*

*And **you** thought we just sold you stuff!*

You

ALPHABETICAL TABLE OF CONTENTS

■ = NEW
▨ = NEWISH

OCTOBER 1995 CATALOGUE

The inside front cover of the REMO catalogue from October 1995

1 2 3 4 5 6 7 8 9 10 11 12 13 14 15 16 17 18 19 20 21 22 23 24 25 26 27 28 29 30 31 32 33 34 35 36 37 38 39 40 41 42 43 44 45 46 47 48 50 51 52 53 54

1988   1995   2013

[49] Failing Big

I have failed many times over the course of my career. With REMO alone I have tried and ultimately failed *five* times. By far the biggest failure was the first one in 1995.

I had always – and as it happens naively – assumed that REMO had become too big and well known to fail. There were too many people who'd invested too much money to let it go down. Also, though REMO had some admin and balance sheet issues, the most important fundamental was strong. There was galloping demand for the merchandise, and incredible loyalty and love [66] for the brand from the people who really mattered, the customers.

But despite all of this, the house of REMO came tumbling down, and it was a pretty big deal. (The administrator would later tell me that he'd never seen a hole that big in a small business. Most fail long before they get to that point, but my persuasive skills are such that I was able to accumulate an impressive amount of unsecured debt. With the benefit of hindsight, it's nothing to be proud of, but I was taking it all on in good faith.)

Colin Seeger was working at Simpsons Solicitors at the time. I remember the conversation. I was in denial up until the very end. I knew that we were cash strapped, but I had always assumed that we would be recapitalised by someone or something with deep pockets, and that everyone would live happily ever after. Colin took me kicking and screaming to visit Alex Linden, an insolvency specialist, who in turn introduced me to Ron Dean-Willcocks, a professional company administrator. I remember Ron sitting me down to tell me that once I set this process in motion, nothing would ever be the same, and that I would find out who my true friends really were. He was right.

The timing was crazy too. "REMO City Ventures Pty Limited" went into Voluntary Administration on the very same day that Melanie gave birth to Lola after a 36-hour labour, an event in itself that would score very highly on any sort of life Richter Scale. I remember being there with Melanie at St Margaret's Hospital in Darlinghurst (as it happens where *I* was born) in a room bursting and sweating with flower arrangements, and having to leave the room occasionally to pace back and forth in the corridor as I fielded calls from newspaper reporters and TV news services. REMO had become an institution in Sydney and no one could believe that it could all come a cropper so quickly.

The business never really recovered from that blow.

Personally, it was *very* tough, and the sense of loss ran dark and deep. I remember my sister Giulia counseling me at one point saying that *"You are not your business."* However, in this case, and given that we shared the name "Remo," it was hard to feel that.

No number of university degrees can really prepare you for the messiness of a fast-growing small business, and in my case the paucity of reliable accounting information and the absence of a clear and controlled path to profitability had proved to be fatal.

It did teach me an important business lesson about fiscal control and the primacy of profitability. Future versions of REMO would fail for reasons of inadequate capitalisation, and **not** for the want of financial information or a defensible business model.

The Sydney Morning Herald   Wednesday, March 22, 1995   3

Style supremo Remo calls in the designer debt squad

Remo Giuffré ... creditors demanding payment.

By IAN VERRENDER

Remo Giuffré, the style king of eastern suburbs chic, yesterday experienced the full meaning of Charles Dickens's line about the best of times and the worst of times.

Just hours after his wife gave birth to their first child, a girl, at St Margaret's Hospital after being in labour for 36 hours, REMO, was placed in the hands of a voluntary administrator.

Hailed as a retailing guru by many of Sydney's arbiters of taste, Giuffré opened his quirky depart-ment store on the corner of Oxford and Crown streets in the late 1980s amid a blaze of publicity.

It was to be the department store of the 1990s, he claimed. REMO subsequently developed a loyal following of well-heeled clients who were prepared to pay a hefty premium on everything from stationery and goanna oil to beeswax candles and boxer shorts.

Australian and New Zealand designers were commissioned to produce a range of products and Japanese department stores began

shipping container loads to a style-hungry Japanese market.

But despite impressive sales performances of 25 per cent compound growth a year, the business racked up a $2 million deficiency in working capital.

With trade creditors baying at the doors, directors of the com-pany yesterday appointed char-tered accountant Ron Dean-Willcocks, of Star Dean Will-cocks, to oversee the operation.

"I have the full support of the board and I hope to have a report for creditors within the next five working days," he told the Herald

yesterday. "We hope to have a deed of arrangement put in place in the near future that will see the company trade its way out of difficulties."

That plan, according to some insiders, will involve the original investors swapping their debt for equity in the company.

In effect, debt has been at the heart of the problem. When he launched the business, Giuffré had no shortage of friends, col-leagues and business acquain-tances to bankroll him into the operation. Many were given the title of "Friends of the Store".

Later fundraisings all were debt-related.

A commerce law graduate from the University of NSW class of '82, Giuffré worked for the estab-lishment law firm Baker & McKenzie before heading to New York and a Master of Business Administration at Columbia Uni-versity. It was then on to cable television and back home to work for Network Media before he hit on the idea of the "mini mini department store".

More recently, Giuffré opened a second store in George Street in the city, although this is run by

another company not under the control of the voluntary adminis-trator. "Basically, the company has been under-capitalised and has been unable to keep up with its own growth," one investor said yesterday. "Remo has been a victim of his own success."

Voluntary administration is a relatively new concept in Austra-lia, effectively bypassing the tradi-tional receivership process. Rather than simply sell off the assets of the business, the adminis-trator attempts to reach a compro-mise with creditors and then trade the company back to good health.

The Sydney Morning Herald, 22 March 1995

Remo on the rebound: stylishly down but not out

By MAGGIE ALDERSON

Visionary retailer Remo Giuffré with his trademark phrenology head and, above left, the Darlinghurst store. Photograph by GLENN HUNT

Remo Giuffré is an Aussie battler in designer clothes. Even though his eponymous landmark Darlinghurst store (it rhymes with demo) is on the brink again, Mr Giuffré's eyes, behind their Buddy Holly spectacles, are fixed firmly on the future.

With the right financier at his side, Mr Giuffré can clearly see Remo as a pan-Australian and, ultimately, international leisure shopping legend. As he points out: "There are more sources of finance than there are of excel-lent shopkeepers."

An inspiring talker and a visionary retailer, his quirky business of unique branded mer-chandise and eclectic classic items grew steadily for more than six years until hitting its first serious speed bump last March.

Despite his second crisis in a year, Mr Giuffré simply does not countenance the idea of a Remo-less Sydney. After all, where else would one buy ironing-board covers featuring the word "Sacrifice" ($36), toy shell headphones ($3.40) and T-shirts featuring the thoughts of Albert Einstein ($32)?

Last March (on the day his daughter, Lola, was born), Remo went into voluntary administration. It looked like the end for our most stylish corner shop – at the junction of Oxford Street and Crown Street in Darlinghurst – but he was saved by a Melbourne-based

retailer, Mr Ken Newton, who bought the "Remo retail oppor-tunity", with an option to open other stores, for $1 million in deferred payments.

Mr Giuffré's problems seemed solved, as did those of his well-heeled customers, 10,000 of them around the world, who couldn't imagine where else they would buy witty, top-quality Christmas presents for their witty, top-quality friends.

Last year, however, saw the speedy opening and closing of a second Remo cafe and store in the CBD. Now Mr Giuffré is seeking another fairy godper-son. The cash injection sought is needed to pay off the creditors that cause the only dent in his buoyant optimism (it is, he says, a matter of personal honour)

and to fund the great move forward, with Melbourne the next venue in sight.

While it may seem bizarre for a business in strife to be planning on expansion, it would help to correct one of the perceived problems with the store – the prices. A pot of Lucas Pawpaw Ointment, for example, is $9 in Remo and $6.75 in Pitt Street's Soul Pattinson. Mr Giuffré explains: "It's a volume issue. We are ordering in the 100s, not the 1,000s, and I won't compromise on quality."

The prices also include the Remo experience of which Mr Giuffré is so proud – the beautiful blue carrier bags, helpful staff and the free gift-wrapping service.

The Sydney Morning Herald, 18 January 1996

REMO sales growth
1988 to 1994

$1M month
December 1993

CRA proposal
March 1995 [82]

With Melanie and Lola at St Margaret's Hospital
in Darlinghurst, 20 March 1995

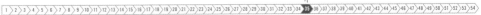
1 2 3 4 5 6 7 8 9 10 11 12 13 14 15 16 17 18 19 20 21 22 23 24 25 26 27 28 29 30 31 32 33 34 35 36 37 38 39 40 41 42 43 44 45 46 47 48 49 50 51 52 53 54

1995

[50] Work Family

Ultimately, it's people who matter. I've always believed that.

I wrote the following in a newsletter included within our November 1991 catalogue:

"The substance of REMO is the collective radiant energy of its people. We can realistically strive to be great and excellent at what we do because we are fortunate enough to have great and passionate people involved at all levels. From a management point of view I regard the attraction and retention of the right people into our enterprise as the single most important factor determining our success at being able to meet our ultimate objectives. Maintaining a positive culture makes for a happy and motivated environment and a helpful, cheerful staff."

The people who worked at REMO during that magical period in the late 80s and early 90s knew they were playing a part in something globally unique and quite remarkable, and they all felt part of a big and modern family. In that same catalogue I paid homage to the stamina of our people and the continuity of our relationships.

For you see, like all good families, we all looked forward to our annual family photograph.

The very first photo was taken a couple of months after the opening of REMO in 1988.

It was designed to create the mock impression that we'd been around for a very long time: labcoats, name badges and sepia tones.

The toilet plunger in my left hand (my sceptre) was chosen to symbolise a commitment to functionality and form over fashion and decoration.

Subsequent photographs took on various themes and involved different people. The memories persist, thanks to the captured images, but also to some souvenirs. The letters from Scrabble REMO (1992) sit in our home in Bondi; and not even in her most frustrated *(Why are we keeping this stuff?)* moment would Melanie suggest that I dispose of the giant fibreglass twiggy letters left over from the Camp REMO shoot of 1994.

The Coco Chanel quote on the Employee Handbook:

*"There's a time for work; and there's a time for love.
That leaves no other time."*

... was also a popular REMO T shirt design.

REMO People 1988 | The Adventure Begins

People with Stamina graphic from the November 1991 REMO Catalogue [43]
along with REMO people images for: 1992, 1993, 1994 and 1995

1 2 3 4 5 6 7 8 9 10 11 12 13 14 15 16 17 18 19 20 21 22 23 24 25 26 27 28 29 30 31 32 33 34 35 36 37 38 39 40 41 42 43 44 45 46 47 48 49 50 51 52 53 54

1988 ◄───► 1995

[51] Au Revoir (Good Buy)

20th Century REMO failed in 1995. It was a big and hairy event [49].

The failure happened for all of the wrong reasons (mismanaged backend, poor information systems, inappropriate high yield *"Friends of the $tore"* junk bond financing), and, paradoxically, at the same time as we were still experiencing high demand for our merchandise and terrific levels of loyalty and love [66] for the REMO brand.

There was a momentary reprieve soon after we hit the wall with the arrival of a white knight from Melbourne who did a deal with Ron Dean-Willcocks, our administrator. As it happens, and later that year, he went broke himself (for reasons unrelated to REMO), taking us back down with him in 1996. But, at the time, there was a glimmer of hope.

I communicated with customers in the only way I know how to, with complete transparency and candour. The cover of that year's promotional mailer carried an image of our head logo [39] sporting a black eye and a bandaid. People appreciated that.

When the white knight defaulted on his obligations to the administrator, REMO slid back into administration and ultimately into liquidation. Ron instructed me to prepare the Darlinghurst store for its final closing down sale, and asked me to think about what the opening discount would be. Most liquidation sales start at 50% off and then that number escalates over time. My response to him (calling on my inner Michael Corleone talking to the Senator about the price he was willing to pay for the gaming licence) was this: *"Zero per cent. I think we should sell everything at 0% off, in other words, for full price."*

I remember the queue on the day that the sale commenced. It went around the block. Despite the hopeful *Au Revoir* message on the Crown Street Window [44], customers had no idea if and when we would ever return. Most of our sales by then were of our own brand, and so people wanted to stockpile their favourites: T shirts, boxer shorts, socks, note pads, shirts or whatever. The administrator was in awe, and, in the face of this remarkable customer support, left scratching his head about why he hadn't had more luck marketing the opportunity to the local business community.

Not all endings are happy, and some outcomes don't make sense. You have to learn to deal with it and be satisfied in the knowledge that you gave it your absolute best.

Hurry, last chance to buy Remo's best – at 0% off

By MAGGIE ALDERSON

Elle and Kylie, Nicole and Tom, Michael and Paula were all customers. Jumper giant Luciano Benetton, television shopping magnate Barry Diller and London-based Janet Holmes à Court shopped there by mail-order.

But not, apparently, enough Sydneysiders.

After several years of struggle, Remo Giuffre has finally been instructed to close the doors of his Darlinghurst corner store.

But not everyone in Sydney will be crying themselves to sleep over the closure.

There have always been the cynics who wondered why one shop, which despite its inflated prices seemed always to be in financial strife, has received so much attention.

Small businesses based more on big ideas than business acumen go broke in Sydney every day. So why should people give an over-priced fig about Remo?

But for the devotees, those who felt defined by its witty epigrammed T-shirts, laundry bags and fetish objects from many lands (Italian soap, English toffee, French beeswax) the Darlinghurst General Store was special.

Opening in 1988, it symbolised the time when Sydney first started to be recognised as a global city of style. Australia has several fashion icons of World Heritage status, and Remo was one of the first, coming after R.M. Williams boots and Drizabones.

Window shopping . . . the closing down display at the cash-strapped store. "It may have been more appreciated overseas than here." Photograph by BEN RUSHTON

With some 15,000 overseas customers on the mailing list for its quirky catalogues, the store achieved something of a cult status among the obsessive consumers of the world's style capitals.

As *Vogue* editor Nancy Pilcher said: "I've had overseas visitors who wanted to visit Remo before anything else in Sydney because they loved the catalogue so much. In some ways I think it may have been more appreciated overseas than here."

For the locals who did shop there, it was a chance to buy into that international fraternity of fabulousness – as in, "Where did you get that fabulous ironing board cover?" They have a couple more weeks to stock up, as Remo is going out with a "0% discount sale", a last chance to stock up on their exclusive own-brand items at full prices.

True devotees will now be able to snap up Remo's final retailing joke. Going out in style, the store has printed a limited-edition commemorative T-shirt. And they are $100 each.

The Sydney Morning Herald, 24 February 1996

| Ouch & Phew, 1995 | Closing down queues | Scrap book by the REMO team presented at farewell drinks at Bayswater Brasserie | Au Revoir postcard February 1996 |

1 2 3 4 5 6 7 8 9 10 11 12 13 14 15 16 17 18 19 20 21 22 23 24 25 26 27 28 29 30 31 32 33 34 35 36 37 38 39 40 41 42 43 44 45 46 47 48 49 50 51 52 53 54

1996

[52] Tucker, Toothpaste & Smile

The beautiful big smile REMO T Shirt design from 1995 (also referenced in our people photograph from that year) has an interesting pedigree.

It was originally lifted from a tube of Italian Kemphor toothpaste by good friend and long-time collaborator Tucker Viemeister in New York.

Tucker's bathroom boasts a FABULOUS global toothpaste collection that is truly something to behold.

A wall of toothpaste tubes, all functional, all easily removed and replaced. Brush your teeth with something different everyday. Genius.

Big Smile with GM Annette Higgins
REMO Bondi, October 2009

Tucker's General Thinker profile
General Thinking [63]

SMILE

1 2 3 4 5 6 7 8 9 10 11 12 13 14 15 16 17 18 19 20 21 22 23 24 25 26 27 28 29 30 31 32 33 34 35 36 37 38 39 40 41 42 43 44 45 46 47 48 49 50 51 52 53 54

1995

[53] Alien of Extraordinary Ability

In 1996 I had one last crack at getting REMO [25] rebooted in Australia, this time from a rented shop front on Bay Street in Double Bay. Once again it didn't work out. Lacking access to any capital, we were unable to fund a mailout in February 1997, despite an extraordinarily high response to a mailout in October 1996. Mini financial meltdown. More pain and embarrassment. Another close shave with personal bankruptcy. Fuck.

We shifted out of our beloved North Bondi apartment, and moved into my Mum's spare bedroom in Edgecliff. Always humbling for a 30-something married man with a family.

I was now *determined* to get my young family to the US, and Melanie (also totally over the conservatism and negativity of the local business environment) was up for it. But, for that to happen, I had to find a company willing to both employ and sponsor me for a working visa. That company turned out to be frog design, an originally German but by then Silicon Valley-based design agency with a handful of offices all over the world. They had a sexy reputation. The founder Hartmut Esslinger had worked with Steve Jobs on the design of the original Macintosh, and this had been followed by a range of high-profile projects.

I became frog's first ever Director of Brand & Strategy, and it became my job (or so I thought) to work across all of the design functions (engineering, industrial design, technology and graphic design) to make sure that everyone's work was congruent and in harmony with the overarching client brand and agreed strategy. But Hartmut was more old fashioned in his thinking, and believed that I belonged more in the graphic design department. We didn't see eye to eye on this, and it was one of the reasons that I left after barely a year to become the Brand Strategist (once again, their first-ever employee with this title) at the pioneering online business builder, Organic. Although based in San Francisco, Organic also had a thriving office in New York, and thankfully my resume was appealing enough to make the shift to New York a condition of my employment. *Woo hoo!* Melanie and I had never really felt at home in the Valley, and we were super excited by that move at the time. So, despite what was now classified as a high-risk pregnancy (having lost Roman's twin at 19 weeks [55]), we packed up our lives once again and headed to the East Coast where we remained for the next three years.

During this sabbatical in the US I learned the following about myself:

1. My skills were transferable and applicable to brands other than my own
2. I was able to function and collaborate within a structured environment
3. I strongly preferred to range freely across functions and resented being siloed

Also, by now, thanks to letters of reference written by some influential people, the US Immigration & Naturalization Service had agreed to regard me as an "Alien of Extraordinary Ability," meaning that I was eligible for permanent residency, and did not need to be sponsored by and tied to any particular US employer.

Ironically, and having worked so hard to get the fabled Green Card, I ultimately never really used it. Our sabbatical concluded when we quite suddenly came to the conclusion that it was time to go home [61].

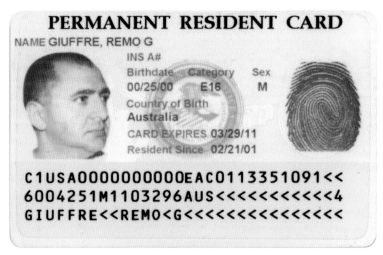

PERMANENT RESIDENT CARD

NAME GIUFFRE, REMO G

INS A#

Birthdate   Category   Sex
00/25/00   E16   M

Country of Birth
Australia

CARD EXPIRES 03/29/11

Resident Since 02/21/01

C1USA0000000000EAC0113351091<<
6004251M1103296AUS<<<<<<<<<<<4
GIUFFRE<<REMO<G<<<<<<<<<<<<<<<

A Green Card for the Alien of Extraordinary Ability

Remo at frog, 1997   Integrated Design   Hartmut Esslinger   Remo at Organic, 1998

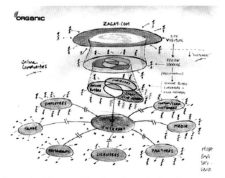

Network of Communities RemoGram for Zagat.com, 1998

1 2 3 4 5 6 7 8 9 10 11 12 13 14 15 16 17 18 19 20 21 22 23 24 25 26 27 28 29 30 31 32 33 34 35 36 37 38 39 40 41 42 43 44 45 46 47 48 49 50 51 52 53 54

1997 - 2001

[54] Relaunch & Reboot | REMO 2.0

The opportunity to scale 20th-Century REMO was mismanaged (mea culpa) ... but, after the initial big failure [49], the only real issue became one of capitalisation. The brand was strong. The demand was proven. The voluntary administration had cleaned up the balance sheet, and the opportunity moving forward was really significant. REMO had legs. Prior to this the problem had been too much development engine and not enough train. We had accumulated the intellectual property ("IP") of a $200m brand on the back of a $5m operating business. The good news was that, although the business was stalled, we had retained the IP for that potential $200m business.

It was disappointing to encounter so little interest in the opportunity in Australia. So, I became increasingly convinced that (sadly) our future was *not* in Australia, and that if REMO was going to fly, it was going to do so from a new capital and operating base in the US, where remote shopping (e.g. mail order) had historically been very strong and where I also knew the immediate future for ecommerce would play out.

So, phoenix-like REMO would rise from the ashes as REMO General Store, Inc. and prove the Australian naysayers wrong. Those fools had no idea. I pitied them.

It took some doing [53] but we ended up getting to the US as a family in 1997. Very soon after arriving I received this email from Steve Tomlin, a loyal REMO customer who was then CEO of a Barry Diller backed decision-making venture called PersonaLogic (subsequently acquired by AOL):

"Our mutual friend Geoffrey Gifford [original REMO store designer and long time Remo collaborator] tells me that you're recently signed on at frogdesign -- congratulations on joining such a great firm. Provided you still have entrepreneurial aspirations in the REMO-branded retail area, however, I have some thoughts that I'd like to discuss with you."

And so it began again: by day I was Clark Kent, a well paid gun for hire brand guru working for high end design firms like frog design and Organic; but by night I was *Superman* working on the reboot and relaunch of REMO 2.0 as a US-based online gift service.

I made a *lot* of progress in a short amount of time. In 1999 I was able to: convince a then venerable Organic to incubate and implicitly endorse the idea (by paying me full time to develop it), engage Rich Kelly from Mintz Levin, a smart and savvy lawyer willing to work on spec, and raise hundreds of thousands of angel-round dollars from some high net worth individuals that included a who's who of US specialty retail: Bill End the CEO of Lands' End, Scott Galloway and Ian Chaplin, the founders of Red Envelope, and others ...

So, what happened?

In early 2000, and at *precisely* the same time that we were starting to pitch for our follow on venture funding, the first Internet bubble burst, and, although very different to companies like pets.com or kozmo.com, REMO 2.0 got painted with the same brush. We never did raise that first-round founding ... and, once again, the REMO General Store tanked.

The lesson? Timing, although not "everything," can *really suck* sometimes.

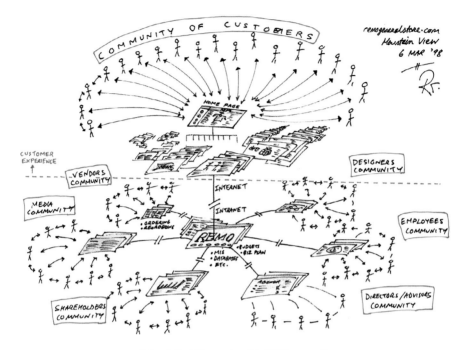

Network Model for a webcentric REMO 2.0, 1998

Steve Tomlin

Randy Komisar

REMO General Store, Inc.
share certificate

Email to angel
investors, 2001

Australian Financial Review
8 November 2000

1 2 3 4 5 6 7 8 9 10 11 12 13 14 15 16 17 18 19 20 21 22 23 24 25 26 27 28 29 30 31 32 33 34 35 36 37 38 39 40 41 42 43 44 45 46 47 48 49 50 51 52 53 54

1996 to 2000

[55] Making Babies

In April 1998 my wife Melanie fell pregnant with Roman. For this joyous event we paid homage at the time to the aggresive-but-effective Pacific Fertility Center in San Francisco, with whom we rolled the dice with our very last $10,000 ... and (frankly) our own dogged faith and persistence.

Making babies did not come easy for us. In fact it was *hell*. It took 15 pregnancies, including six heart-breaking tear-jerking miscarriages and, in the latter years, quite a few failed IVF cycles, to yield our two precious children: Lola and Roman.

Moreover this baby-making included four ectopic pregnancies. That's when the fertilised egg gets stuck in a fallopian tube instead of moving down to its rightful place in the uterus. When that happens things can also get dangerous for the mother. Melanie's first ectopic pregnancy happened soon after we got engaged in 1991 [38], and the others after Lola was born; hence the IVF requirement for Roman.

Check out below litany of woes from a form letter sent to friends and family in March 1997.

This kind of life experience can make or break a marriage at the best of times; but when overlaid with some extraordinary business stresses, the surviving relationship becomes all the more remarkable.

PS: We have been blessed with two healthy kids. The other good thing that came from all of this was a nice piece of family jewellery. In 1994 I commissioned Brisbane jeweller Barbara Heath (the maker of our wedding rings) to make us a fertility charm, possibly feeling at this point that a little bit of magic wouldn't go astray. The brief was very open. Essentially it had to work! Barby had been wanting to use seed pearls in something for some time; and the paisley shape was also her idea.

¶ **1995**
- March 1995: – REMO (business) falters for the 1st time — Bad
- Lola Born: 20 March 1995 — **Wonderful**
- July 1995: REMO rescued by "white knight" — Temporary Relief
- December 1995: The white knight goes under — Bad

¶ **1996**
- REMO falters for the 2nd time. Store closes/liquidation. — Bad
- Melanie has ectopic pregnancy #2 — Bad
- Melanie's business falters –> liquidation. R&M broke. — Bad
- Remo & Melanie & Lola move in with Remo's mother — Appreciated
- Melanie suffers ectopic pregnancy #3 — Bad
- Remo/REMO relaunches MAIL ORDER SERVICE — Good
- REMO reopens tiny Store & makes small profit — Good

¶ **1997**
- Melanie endures ectopic pregnancy #4 — Bad
- Slow January for fragile REMO. Cash flow crisis looms. — Bad
- Remo decides to search for a REMO business partner — Long Overdue
- Remo gives himself even chance of doing deal in time — Realistic
- Bruno (brother) & Sonia (sister) both have thyroids out — Bad –> Relieving
- Remo continuing to fight small legal fires from past — Time Wasting
- Lola approaches 2, a total delight and coming on a treat — Very Good

You get the picture?

From a letter to friends and family, March 1997

BIG SISTER
EOLA *"LOLA"* JESSICA GIUFFRÉ
CRADLES

ROMAN VINCENT EOLO GIUFFRÉ
()
BORN IN NEW YORK CITY
23 DECEMBER 1998 ~ 7LBS 3.5OZ

FIFTEEN PREGNANCIES. TWO CHILDREN. ONE OF EACH.
THAT'S PRETTY MUCH IT FOR US.

NEW LIFE AT HOME
NEW YORK CITY ~ FEBRUARY 1999

New year card to friends and family, February 1999

Fertility charm

Barby at work in her studio
Photo: Chelsea Sipthorp

Melanie
models it

Lola and Roman
July 2014

Roman's US
passport

[56] Network Model

Theories and ideas are well and good, but there's nothing more satisfying than a diagram that brings it all together.

Since my teens I had been instinctively respectful of the marketplace power of networking e.g. the only way I was able to sell all of those tickets to the 1980 Aqua-Ball [12] was by virtue of the customer-get-customer system that was a feature of my Aqua-Packs.

The most powerful empirical evidence for the network model that I had intuited and organically developed over the years was demonstrated by the impressive year-on-year growth of the REMO General Store from 1988 to 1994 (50% compounded from a single store), and that was when it was 100% offline, where it is much harder for customers to manifest the relevant referral and participatory behaviours.

In 1999 I was living in New York and trying to attract venture capital to the exclusively online version of REMO. I had angel round funding in place, but it was all going to come to nought if I was unable to secure follow on first round funding from venture capitalists. And, for that to happen, I needed to demonstrate a unique and defensible business model. I found myself in a position of having to articulate the underlying structures and the thing that was going to make this different to all other high margin niche retailers.

So I developed this sequence of diagrams to communicate my beloved Network Model. It was an exciting visualisation breakthrough. I did (and still do) feel that this was a next generation business model that exhibits radically different characteristics from those seen in the traditional marketplace. A networked organisational structure facilitates the meaningful involvement of customers in certain processes, most critically, development and marketing. The customer network becomes both the development engine and the marketing engine for the brand and the business.

Not B2C › **B=C**

The Community is The Brand

It really is a better mousetrap for any customer-facing business.

PS: See also [30], [32], [47] and [60]

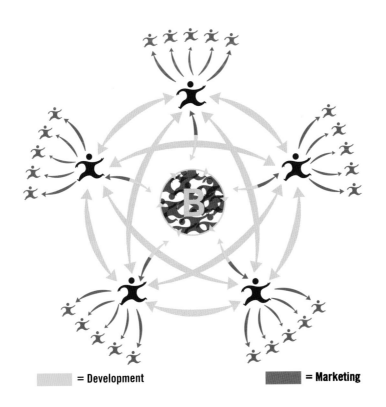

Network Model sequence of RemoGrams, 1999

Business model outcomes

Network marketing [57]

Better mousetrap

1 2 3 4 5 6 7 8 9 10 11 12 13 14 15 16 17 18 19 20 21 22 23 24 25 26 27 28 29 30 31 32 33 34 35 36 37 38 39 40 41 42 43 44 45 46 47 48 49 50 51 52 53 54

1999

[57] Customer Sponsorship

The best source of new customers is via an existing network of delighted customers, whereby *they* become the low-cost marketing engine for the brand and the business [56].

The growth in the REMO customer network was always driven by referral and sponsorship, because we focused all of our energies on just two things:

1. Serving, delighting and rewarding our existing customers
2. Enabling and encouraging them to "sponsor" new customers

Over the years we developed all sorts of one-click ways to enable our customers to tell their friends about us, and this was all pre-social media.

From as early as 2002 each logged-in REMO customer had an online control panel from which they could generate individual or group emails to people whom they thought might like to join the "REMOlution." For each sponsorship they sent out, a customer was rewarded with REMO Points, which accumulated to accrue "Very Special Customer" status. If their friend ended up joining, the sponsoring customer earned a whole lot more points. Once their friend joined, the relationship with the sponsoring customer was made visible on the website ... and people could click back to see who begat whom. In this way the genealogy of the customer network was both documented and celebrated, just like a big family tree. It's a technique that I have more recently replicated for the development of the General Thinking [63] network.

The customer sponsorship process worked well for REMO. By mid-2011 the 90 email addresses that we were able to salvage from our 20th-Century mailing list had spawned a network of around 40,000 customers in over 110 countries.

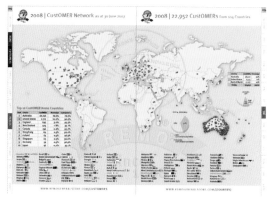

REMO 2008 Printed Thing, Pages 104 and 105

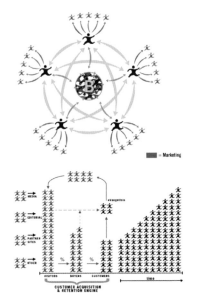

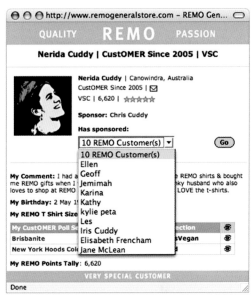

Customer sponsors earned REMO Points and became Very Special CustOMERs ("VSC")

NEW → **CUSTOMER** → **VSC**

VSCs were stars

VSC keyring

Typical VCS gifts

Looking after the VSCs

Workin' it

1 2 3 4 5 6 7 8 9 10 11 12 13 14 15 16 17 18 19 20 21 22 23 24 25 26 27 28 29 30 31 32 33 34 35 36 37 38 39 **40** 41 42 43 44 45 46 47 48 49 50 51 52 53 54

2000

[58] Customers are Smart

If you're standing in a store, browsing the pages of this book and thinking about whether or not to buy it, please note the price that has been set by the retailer. If it ends in the numbers 95 or (heaven forbid) 99, then *please* insist that the price be rounded up to the next dollar. We must not encourage them further by playing along with their silly game.

Prices like $29.99 have always been verboten in my businesses. The messaging is really *bad* ... and frankly I don't care if the research proves me wrong. Whatever financial benefits may accrue do nothing to counter the damage suffered by the brand.

Similarly, I don't like the word "consumers." It implies a passivity that is at odds with the level of engagement that I think we should be aspiring to achieve with our customers.

I have always been a big believer in the intelligence of customers. Here's what I wrote under the heading "Smart Customers" in the REMO newsletter from November 1991:

*"At the bottom of all of our plans & actions is an assumption that our customers (i.e. **you**) are smart people. This isn't idle flattery. It's common sense – and the basis of our whole business. If we treat you like idiots, you're going to shop somewhere else. We're succeeding where other supposedly experienced retailers are struggling. And this success is not so much a credit to our cleverness. The really smart thing we did was to base our business on the assumption that **our customers** were smart."*

This assumption was also made manifest by the sophistication of our merchandising. It was never necessary for everyone to get the joke on every occasion e.g. it was mostly the physicists and geeks who were buying our *Heisenberg* T shirt design. We made things challenging so our customers knew we had nothing but respect for them.

In the April 2004 issue of New York's PAPER Magazine, the industrial designer Tucker Viemeister [52] referred to REMO as *"the Einstein of stores,"* and I must say that, as a longtime Albert fan, I was very pleased with the comparison.

BRC #017, August 2009

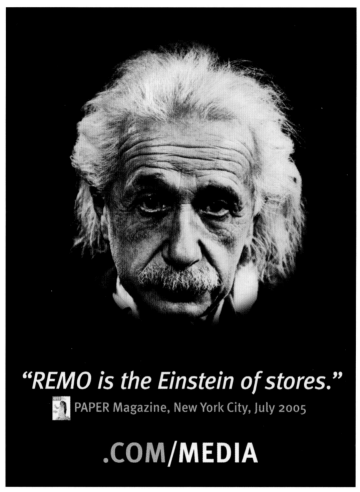

"*REMO is the Einstein of stores.*"

PAPER Magazine, New York City, July 2005

.COM/MEDIA

REMO Bondi Road Corner Poster, August 2009

Puh-lease

REMO Crown Street Window
Evolution of a CustOMER, 1992

Nov 1991
newsletter

Heisenberg T shirt
design, 1993

PAPER
July 2005

1 2 3 4 5 6 7 8 9 10 11 12 13 14 15 16 17 18 19 20 21 22 23 24 25 26 27 28 29 30 31 32 33 34 35 36 37 38 39 40 41 42 43 44 45 46 47 48 49 50 51 52 53 54

1988   2005 2009

[59] Lonelyville

There's a special place that means a lot to me. You might be interested to learn about it.

It used to be the case that anyone who could afford to leave New York over the summer would do so, often heading to the Hamptons or some other beach-side community.

Early on in our time living in New York as a family we discovered Fire Island. It's closer to New York than the Hamptons (the ferry port at Bayshore is only an hour by train from Pennsylvania Station) and yet mysteriously overlooked as a destination by most New Yorkers … probably because of its reputation as a gay enclave. Indeed, it is best known for its vibrant gay communities, The Pines and Cherry Grove. However, there are all manner of other community flavours on the island, ranging from regular Joe (Ocean Beach) to waspy (Point O'Woods) to teetotalling (Saltair) to liberal/intellectual (Fairharbour/Dunewood).

The community that *we* discovered and aligned with was called Lonelyville. How could you *not* love a place with a name like that? One notable Lonelyville resident Bob Greenberg (Mel Brooks was another), the founder of the global R/GA digital agency, is a long-time TEDster whose business card listed the three places in the US that he called home: Hell's Kitchen, Death Valley and Lonelyville. Very cool. For a brand guy like me, this place ticked all the boxes.

For a time Melanie and I owned a home within this tiny beach-side enclave at 59 Shell Walk. It was the first piece of property that we had ever managed to buy together, a ramshackle place with rotting wooden decks and an illegal roof terrace … and we loved it.

What we also loved was the nature and quality of the life on Fire Island. It was a salty and sandy place with no cars, the Atlantic Ocean in your face, and clammy sand between your toes. Kids ran feral up and down the island doing all sorts of cliched 50s things: swimming, fishing, canoeing, collecting shells, making things, setting up little stands to sell those things. It was a very safe environment. People got around either by foot or on push bikes, and everyone used little red wagons to move their stuff. Classic *Radio Flyers* were the norm, but there were other more deluxe versions. One anniversary gift to Melanie was a wooden wagon from the Wisconsin Wagon Company bearing the name GIUFFRE carved into the back. We still have it.

The reason we loved that life on Fire Island so much is that it reminded us of life in Australia. It had that super casual, bare-footed, spontaneous vibe about it … and for this utopia to exist so near to Manhattan was, to us, extraordinary.

Along with the wagon and a bunch of clam shells that we still use as candle holders, my favourite bit of Fire Island memorabilia is a framed copy of a page from the *The New York Times* from 28 May 2000. There in a photograph captioned *To Get to the Beach, Take the Sea Train* is the unmistakably buxom form of Melanie walking down the stairs of Penn Station, with me not far behind schlepping a pram containing Roman. Ergo, we can actually say that our photos have appeared on the front page of *The New York Times*.

Lonelyville, Fire Island, 2001

Remo

The New York Times, 28 May 2000

Melanie

1 2 3 4 5 6 7 8 9 10 11 12 13 14 15 16 17 18 19 20 21 22 23 24 25 26 27 28 29 30 31 32 33 34 35 36 37 38 39 40 41 42 43 44 45 46 47 48 49 50 51 52 53 54

2001

[60] The Community is the Brand

S.P.Q.R. Senatus Populusque REMO

Given that the name "Remo" is derived from "Remus" (one of Rome's wolf-sucking and co-founding twins) I'm surely allowed to appropriate this august Roman acronym.

This one-page overview for the online REMO General Store from 2000 communicated the fact that the development of the brand moving forward would need to involve a visible customer network, the development happening online and in full view of all participants. The process would be transparent. That would keep things: honest, collaborative, efficient, communicative, unique, and, most of all … FUN!

The RemoGram overview was a manifestation of my 1999 Network Model [56].

It was also the first opportunity for me to really push the new "Global Community General Store" tagline, four words that summarised with great economy (albeit in reverse order of chronology) the journey of discovery that I had been on since launching REMO in 1988 i.e.

1988: **Store**
Learning that a retail store could front a values-driven communications business

1990: **General** Store
Utilising and modifying the positioning of a warm and cosy *ye olde* general store

1991: **Community** General Store
Appreciating the key development and marketing roles played by the customer community

1995: **Global** Community General Store
Realising that an online community is de facto global, enabling a niche business to scale

I was proud of the diagram's ability to encapsulate what I was proposing. So much so that I made a T shirt (dipping into precious archival blank REMO stock) bearing the image across the chest. I actually wore it to a couple of meetings with venture capitalists, thereby effectively *wearing* the REMO 2.0 business model as I entered their meeting rooms.

Finally, there are a couple of other things to note about this RemoGram:

1. Merchandise Iceberg [33] snuck into the top right hand corner
2. Café [85] icon at the centre and representative of the whole communications piece

It all made sense, but this Sharon Aris comment in *The Bulletin* magazine article entitled "Community Consumption" supporting the business model was portentous [54]:

"Giuffré is indisputably an optimist: close in Sydney, relaunch from New York; shut a catalogue in 1997, launch an online community in 2000 – all in the months after the big IT stockmarket correction in the United States."

REMO® GLOBAL COMMUNITY GENERAL STORE℠
BETA SCHEMATIC ~ 25 APRIL 2000

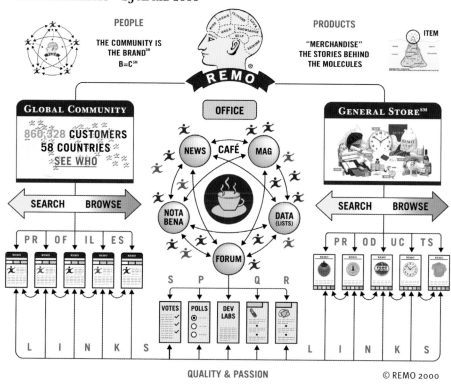

PEOPLE

THE COMMUNITY IS
THE BRAND℠

B=C℠

PRODUCTS

"MERCHANDISE"
THE STORIES BEHIND
THE MOLECULES

ITEM

REMO

GLOBAL COMMUNITY

OFFICE

GENERAL STORE℠

860,328 CUSTOMERS
58 COUNTRIES
SEE WHO

NEWS   CAFÉ   MAG

NOTA
BENA

DATA
(LISTS)

FORUM

SEARCH   BROWSE

SEARCH   BROWSE

PR   OF   IL   ES

PR   OD   UC   TS

S   P   Q   R

VOTES   POLLS   DEV
LABS

L   I   N   K   S

L   I   N   K   S

QUALITY & PASSION

© REMO 2000

The Bulletin
August 2008

REMO®

GLOBAL COMMUNITY GENERAL STORE℠

Remo Giuffré

VOICEMAIL & FAX: +1 (212) 894 3700 ~ EXT. 1802
EMAIL: REMO@REMOGENERALSTORE.COM

THE GATHERING ~ 2000
WWW.REMOGENERALSTORE.COM/RG.CFM

Yet another Remo business card

With Roman in Lonelyville
wearing the RemoGram

1 2 3 4 5 6 7 8 9 10 11 12 13 14 15 16 17 18 19 20 21 22 23 24 25 26 27 28 29 30 31 32 33 34 35 36 37 38 39 40 41 42 43 44 45 46 47 48 49 50 51 52 53 54

2000

[61] Australia HOME

Melanie and I have done a fair bit of moving around in our lives. I've lived in New York twice, once as an MBA student for a few years in the mid 80s and then with my young family in the late 90s. Melanie's equivalent "other" city is Paris. She left Adelaide when she was 19, did some modelling throughout South East Asia and ended up in Paris ... where she stayed for 5 years, running a business representing hair and make-up artists and photographers. She would ultimately relocate and reboot this business in Sydney in 1987 as Melanie Dames Agency [8].

20th-Century REMO faltered at around the same time that the Age of the Internet was arriving, and I became fixated with the notion that REMO, if it came back, would be better off relaunched as an online business serving a global community from a new capital and operating base in the US. Thanks to my REMO international customer and TEDster networks, I knew enough people there to help make it all happen. I just needed to get **us** up there somehow. In 1997, mostly for financial reasons, we were back living with my mother in Edgecliff. During this time I went for a scouting trip to the US to try to find a job that would sponsor me for a working visa, thereby enabling me to shift the family.

I interviewed at News Corporation, Microsoft, Starbucks, and with a bunch of the interactive agencies that were beginning to establish themselves on the back of a growing Web 1.0 wave. Every positive job interview had Melanie imagining us living in a different city. (*"Microsoft went well? Ooh, Seattle sounds nice."*) She wasn't particularly fussed re location, although, much to my chagrin, she didn't want it to be New York. (As an aside ... that would later change. After a year living an isolated and disconnected life in the suburbs of Silicon Valley, where it really felt like we were both living on some kind of witness protection programme, New York became the ONLY place she wanted to live.) Anyway, in that first instance, I ended up getting a job at frog design as their first-ever Brand Strategist. frog were based in Sunnyvale, and we ended up renting a bungalow in Mountain View.

We moved to New York in 1998. We lived in TriBeCa. We made a life there. Roman was born, and we three became four. New York really did feel like home ... until it didn't.

In 2001 we renewed our vows to Sydney and made the decision that Australia was going to be our family's HOME. We still loved New York ... but we didn't need to live there.

I designed this Australia HOME T shirt for my friend Peter Holmes à Court who, not long before this, had made a similar decision (which, as an aside, he has for the moment reversed).

It was a popular REMO design, and sold very strongly through the online store, as well as via various airport kiosks here in Sydney. It reminds me that you can live in a lot of places, but usually there's only one place that, at any one time, you can really call home.

Australia HOME, 2001

Australia HOME
T shirt design

Peter Holmes à
Court the Rabbitoh

Claudia Karvan and
Cate Blanchett

Home is Bondi ... at
the beach [23]

Bondi Icebergs [88]
wearing Cole [73]

1 2 3 4 5 6 7 8 9 10 11 12 13 14 15 16 17 18 19 20 21 22 23 24 25 26 27 28 29 30 31 32 33 34 35 36 37 38 40 41 42 43 44 45 46 47 48 49 50 51 52 53 54

2002

[62] Chapters of Life

When we moved to New York in the late 90s, we had thought it to be a permanent move. Indeed I had managed to get a Green Card [53], and our son Roman was born there.

I was working at the time as a consultant brand strategist, getting freelance work here and there ... but not quite enough. Once again we were starting to go backwards financially, and, with the cost of living in New York being what it is, when that starts happening, it happens really *fast*.

For that and some other family reasons we decided in 2001 to move back to Sydney. Like most big life decisions that Melanie and I have made over the years, we made it intuitively and we made it very, very quickly.

How would Lola our six-year old daughter react? Eola (the technically accurate name she chose to use while we lived in the US) was happily ensconced within a remarkable school in Greenwich Village called City & Country. She had lots of friends in the neighbourhood. She was happy in New York, and had been only two when we left Sydney in 1997.

We decided to break the news to her over Saturday brunch at her favourite neighbourhood restaurant (Odeon [37] in TriBeCa). The night before I made this RemoGram as a way of explaining to her how all of these geographic moves just signified the progression for all of us collectively and individually from one "life chapter" to the next.

The brunch began and the food started to appear. Nervously, and at an opportune moment, I revealed the RemoGram. As soon as Melanie saw it appear, she burst into tears. Naturally. I explained to Lola what it all meant ... and the decision that Melanie and I had made.

She looked at the two of us, cracked her serene Lola'esque Mona Lisa smile and said this:

"OK ... and could you please pass me the orange juice."

The lesson?

Kids are often more resilient that you think they are, and if you're able to create a strong enough family unit, it doesn't really matter where you decide to live, or how often you decide to move.

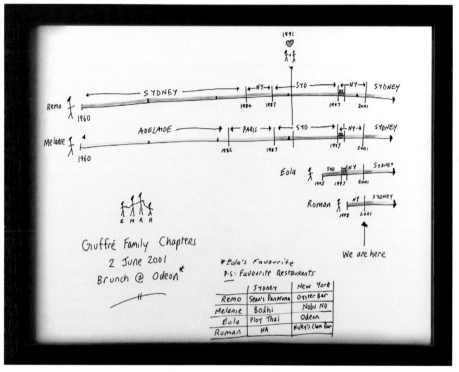

Chapters of Life RemoGram, New York City, 2 June 2001

Lola with blocks

Lola and Roman in 2001

The Odeon Restaurant

Odeon ticket dispensed on the day from the machine at the front door

Farewell Eola poster

1 2 3 4 5 6 7 8 9 10 11 12 13 14 15 16 17 18 19 20 21 22 23 24 25 26 27 28 29 30 31 32 33 34 35 36 37 38 39 40 41 42 43 44 45 46 47 48 49 50 51 52 53 54

2001

[63] General Thinking

General Thinking is a global network of thinkers and doers: creative, wise and engaged; thoughtful people doing good work.

The primary *raison d'être* for the General Thinking Network is simply to BE ... a networking platform and a source of support, inspiration and opportunity for its own members.

It's my newest project. I'm having a lot of fun with it, and I think it could actually be turning into something very special and quite valuable for all involved.

Back in 2000 I was still living in New York. The NASDAQ had crashed and the Web 1.0 bubble had burst, leaving REMO 2.0 [54] and its angel investors high and dry without the follow on venture funding needed to turn an online prototype into a fully back-ended business.

Even so, the fundraising process had forced me to think through and articulate an underlying referral-driven Network Model [58] and so now I was curious to validate my ideas by applying that model to a new brand for which there would be no prior association (as there had been with the highly regarded REMO brand).

And so in early 2001, with longtime collaborator Geoffrey Gifford, I founded General Thinking (i.e. **Thinking** born of my experiences with the REMO **General** Store) ... as a social networking experiment. It was something that we could work on without the need for capital. The beta version began as an online manifestation of my own personal network of creative collaborators, which then developed, via a then unique process of nomination and endorsement, to include a diverse collection of individuals from all over the world; people thinking clear thoughts and doing good work: designers, writers, architects, artists, entrepreneurs, directors, journalists, chefs, scientists, sociologists and musicians ... an online "guild", a band of brothers and sisters. It actually worked a treat, but in those days (pre-Friendster, pre-LinkedIn, pre-Facebook) we had less of an idea of what to DO with it, and how to make it sustainable ... and so, soon after I returned to Sydney in late 2001, it fizzled out for want of a function, and due to my need to focus on financial survival.

Fast forward more than a decade. Two "special projects" that I was working on: a global networked cafés project [81] and TEDxSydney [75], both called for the application of a broad range of skills and wisdom. So, in 2013, I decided that it was time to reform the group, this time with help from web developer and close collaborator, Adam Dennis [84] (aka General Thinker #3).

The idea is to recapture the original essence of General Thinking, to rebuild the global network ... but this time with developing plans to DO, rather than just BE.

Finally, it's no accident that the manifesto for General Thinking begins and ends with the central tenets of my personal motto: *Do Good Work. Have Some Fun.*

PS: Do Good Work [68]

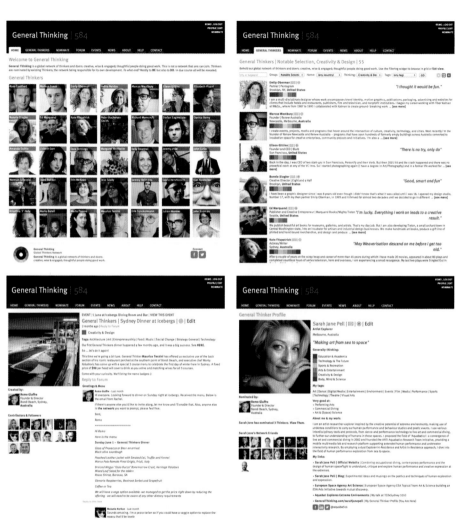

Screen Shots from the General Thinking website, July 2014

General Thinker lapel pin
and numbered keyring

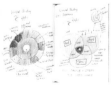

General Thinking RemoGrams,
4 September 2013

1 2 3 4 5 6 7 8 9 10 11 12 13 14 15 16 17 18 19 20 21 22 23 24 25 26 27 28 29 30 31 32 33 34 35 36 37 38 39 40 41 42 43 44 45 46 47 48 49 50 51 52 53 54

2001   2013

[64] Returning to Sydney

In 2001, having decided as a family to return home [61] to Sydney, we crammed the contents of our TriBeCa loft into a shipping container and packed ourselves up to spend our final North American summer at our house on Fire Island in Lonelyville [59]. We had to sell that house to fund this transition and the trip back home, but the settlement wasn't happening for a while.

That summer was a happy and relaxed time. I spent a bit of time thinking about what the hell I was going to be doing next to support my family … but mostly it was about saying goodbye to our New York friends, and enjoying that extraordinary Fire Island environment. I collected many shells and did lots of crafty things.

Summer came to an end and it was time to go home. Our Qantas flight out of JFK was delayed due to the wild weather, but we ultimately took our plane back to Sydney via LA.

We boarded on 10 September 2001, and disembarked in Sydney on the 12th. I don't have to tell you what happened while we were suspended somewhere between LA and Sydney.

I don't think that our pilots had any clue. Lola and Roman had a cockpit tour toward the very end of the flight. Remember those? Would this have been allowed had the pilots been aware of what had gone down in New York? I doubt it.

After we landed, and while still on the tarmac, we were told what had happened. It didn't sound credible. We had lived quite literally in the shadows of those towers and there was no way to easily imagine their "total destruction."

We were greeted at the airport by our good friend Peter Holmes à Court. Peter knew what we were in for, and was looking to protect us from the media scrum. But his shepherding skills, although prodigious, were not enough to save me from the Channel 9 News reporter, and so there I was later that night on the six o'clock news, trying to articulate a reaction to the unfolding tragedy. A LOT of Australians saw that news report. So much for the quiet re-entry.

Along with the shock and horror, and over time, Melanie and I experienced a certain amount of regret that we weren't able to be with our friends in New York to share that 9/11 aftermath experience.

In many respects we had dodged a bullet with some surreal timing. On the other hand, we had narrowly missed out on an opportunity to pull together and bond with a community of New Yorkers at a level that is rare and ultimately life affirming.

REMO, MELANIE, LOLA & ROMAN GIUFFRÉ

To travel hopefully is a better thing than to arrive,
and the true success is to labour.

ROBERT LOUIS STEVENSON

After 4 wonderful years of life in the US, we decided in June
(suddenly and as usual instinctively) to pack it all up and
shift the base of the family back to Sydney for the next leg
of our "journey." We took off from JFK in New York on
10 September 2001. We landed in Sydney on 12 September.
The world changed while we were in the air.

We actually left our New York loft 6 weeks earlier and took
precious time to reflect by the beach in Lonelyville on Fire
Island (where this family photo was taken by a friend).
Lasting memories and such a great good bye. (Au Revoir?)

In Sydney we live in a house with a view of another ocean.
Enjoying this latest leg and thinking of you all.

Cheers & Love

BACK IN SYDNEY

5 SEAVIEW STREET WAVERLEY NSW 2024 AUSTRALIA
SYDNEY HOME TELEPHONE: +61 (2) 9369 5600

REMO: +61 (0) 418 18 36 32 | REMO@GENERALTHINKING.COM
MELANIE: +61 (0) 418 18 33 86 | MELANIEG@ONEBOX.COM

COMING SOON: WWW.REMOGENERALSTORE.COM

Lonelyville Beach portrait and card to friends and family, January 2002

The Sydney Morning Herald, April 2002

1 2 3 4 5 6 7 8 9 10 11 12 13 14 15 16 17 18 19 20 21 22 23 24 25 26 27 28 29 30 31 32 33 34 35 36 37 38 39 40 41 42 43 44 45 46 47 48 49 50 51 52 53 54

2001

[65] Intelligent Life Online

I met Randy Komisar [54] in the 90s on one of my buying trips to San Francisco. Then in 1997, soon after I moved to Silicon Valley, we reconnected to talk through the possibility of relaunching REMO from a new capital and operating base in the US. Randy, who is today a partner at the venture capital firm Kleiner Perkins Caufield Byers, was operating at the time as a "Virtual CEO" for a range of valley start ups, a unique role that was subsequently documented in a Harvard Business School case study. He was a maverick and a gun. The idea was that he was going to help me connect with the right people on Sand Hill Road.

I lent Randy some of the old REMO catalogues. He sent them back declaring that:

"REMO was an online brand before there was an online."

It was nice to receive the validation from someone so plugged in, but it was something that I already knew … and in fact had known before I was really in the position to know.

In November 1991 I wrote this in a customer catalogue, after recounting the problem that my friend Katy Foster was having finding somewhere decent to rent in Potts Point:

"We see this as the ultimate service. Enabling our mailing list members and customers to communicate with one another by virtue of their shared relationship with the Store. The potential is great. One day this notice board could operate to link Sydney Store customers of future REMO Stores in other cities throughout the world. There's no real difference between the search for a one bedroom flat in Potts Point and the desire to rent out a country house in Tuscany for the month of June. The future then brings with it something of a "global notice board" – for exclusive use by you as customers of REMO."

So, you can see why, when the Internet came along I fell to my knees in gratitude to the gods of technology. The Internet was going to be able to let us create and serve a global community of customers with services and experiences that would have been very hard to deliver offline.

REMO went online in 1994 … and stayed there until 2012. It was fun while it lasted.

Enjoy the walk down home page memory lane on the facing page.

Final day screen shots of REMOGENERALSTORE.COM, 30 April 2012

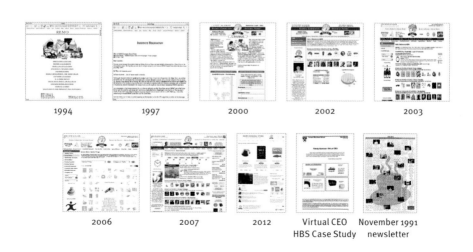

1994

1997

2000

2002

2003

2006

2007

2012

Virtual CEO
HBS Case Study

November 1991
newsletter

1 2 3 4 5 6 7 8 9 10 11 12 13 14 15 16 17 18 19 20 21 22 23 24 25 26 27 28 29 30 31 32 33 34 35 36 37 38 39 40 41 42 43 44 45 46 47 48 49 50 51 52 53 54

1994 ← → 2012

[66] Lovemark

A good thing happened at the end of 2003.

The REMO General Store was nominated by one of our customers to be classified as a "lovemark" (defined by global ad agency Saatchi & Saatchi and its CEO Worldwide Kevin Roberts to be a brand that inspires "loyalty beyond reason.").

Also, we have been featured in both Lovemarks books published to date.

Somewhat paradoxically, the REMO General Store is still ranked **#16** on the Top 200 Lovemarks list online, despite the fact that it hasn't actually traded since 2012.

So, what was the reason for all of this extraordinary customer love?

I have some theories:

We didn't set out in 1988 with a master plan for REMO to generate love and "loyalty beyond reason." However, those two things are natural by-products of: how I instinctively communicated [20], the way we did things and (critically) the network model [56] underpinning how we were structured. We involved customers in our business processes, most especially the development and marketing functions. In this way "The Community is the Brand" and our customers felt a real sense of ownership and pride in the brand that they were helping to develop and make great. The other thing that set us apart was the nature of our business mission. Selling stuff was never our *raison d'être*; and yet, paradoxically, it's the selling of stuff that fueled the development of the brand in pursuance of a vision. Customers were really able to feel this distinction.

Loyalty for REMO was driven by a sense of belonging to the REMO community and overall gestalt. It's a tribal thing. People feel connected, and the fact that our customer network was global added a certain cachet and mystery. This loyalty manifested itself in many ways. Customers told others about us. They forgave us our mistakes (and there were many). They defaulted to us for their gift purchasing [78] wherever possible. They supported the team.

There are dozens of testimonials appearing on the Lovemarks website. Take a look.

Kevin's Lovemark idea on a napkin
(A man after my own heart)

REMO General Store

First nominated 9 November 2003 by Stan Jarin, Australia

REMO was launched in Sydney Australia in 1988 as a general store
with a mission to seek out and celebrate Quality & Passion in people
and merchandise gathered together from all over the world.

previous: REI | next: ROLO Ice Cream

LOSE IT	LOVE IT!
68	1594

REMO General Store Links
www.remogeneralstore...

Videos for REMO General Store:

There are currently no REMO General Store videos

SUBMIT A VIDEO >

Comments

1 to 10 (of 48)

Love Is...

REMO is the antithesis of blah, an online Aladdin's cave, the essence of must have and always, but always.....fun. It's a reminder of a misspent youth, the excitement of providing the perfect gift and knowing that the recipient will not be able to resist REMO-ing in return. Love is a REMO stripey thing.

Marcia, Australia - 19 November 2003

To Give And To Receive

In a world full of "throw-away" items REMO's own brand is quite unique ... the quality is unsurpassed and the designs are timeless. One of their captions is "buy it once, own it forever" and the goods live up to the slogan. To give a gift from Remo is a guaranteed hit, to receive one an absolute delight.

James, Australia - 29 January 2004

Places & Times Long Forgotten

Remo is a Tardus that transports me back to places & times long forgotten, and holds promise of yet-to-be-imagined new delights.

Tracy, Australia - 19 November 2003

With A Passion

I love REMO, coz REMO loves me. Its as simple as that... I love every single REMO item I have ever owned or gifted with a passion. Yeah.

Megan, New Zealand - 08 January 2004

Add to my Lovemarks
Comment on this Lovemark
Share a Lovemarks story

REMO General Store and the community...

Members who love it:
Alan James, Australia
st martins, Australia
Sean Hawkridge, United Kingdom

SEE ALL >

Members who love REMO General Store also love:
Moleskine
Helvetica
Moleskine

The REMO General Store page at Lovemarks.com, July 2014

REMO Logo [39]
love segment

Kevin Roberts
Saatchi & Saatchi

LOVE Sign by Al
James, 2004

Printed Thing
2008

BRC #040
February 2011

[67] Lola's Daisy Chain

"Sculpture by the Sea" is the world's largest outdoor free-to-the-public exhibition of contemporary sculpture, staged along Sydney's spectacular Bondi to Tamarama coastal walk each October/November. Each year the exhibition, which attracts over 500,000 visitors, exhibits approximately 100 works by artists from Australia and overseas. It has become a Sydney institution … a joyous celebration of coastal creativity!

In 2004 our then nine-year-old daughter Lola decided that she wanted to submit something for that year's event. At the time we lived in a rented house at Tamarama, overlooking the coastal walk, and Melanie would often take Lola on walks to pick the daisies.

For Sculpture by the Sea, the Daisy Chain was her first idea … and what an idea.

The chain of 35,000 custom-made polyester silk daisies, the purchase of which was underwritten by her Godfather Dare Jennings [21] and supported by friends and family, ran the entire 1.5km stretch, extending from the south end of Tamarama Beach … all the way to the Bondi Icebergs, and thanks to my long relationship with restaurateur Maurice Terzini, actually all the way through the iconic Icebergs Dining Room and Bar.

The project involved hundreds of people and thousands of hours. It became a real local community endeavour.

The experience taught Lola a valuable lesson, and reminded us all that a good idea is only part of the story. Execution is also crucial, and that execution usually involves a lot of effort from many people.

To celebrate Lola's Daisy Chain we naturally produced a REMO T shirt which faithfully quotes words from her Artist's Statement:

"I like daisy chains because you start with something little, and end up with something big."

I like daisy chains because
you start with something little, and
end up with something big.

LOLA GIUFFRÉ
DAISY CHAIN: BONDI TO TAMARAMA
SCULPTURE BY THE SEA 2004

1 2 3 4 5 6 7 8 9 10 11 12 13 14 15 16 17 18 19 20 21 22 23 24 25 26 27 28 29 30 31 32 33 34 35 36 37 38 39 40 41 42 43 **44** 45 46 47 48 49 50 51 52 53 54

2004

[68] Do Good Work

Good work is its own reward.

The people I enjoy working with are those for whom this maxim holds true. They don't care how many versions are required to get things right, and they are also aware there's really no such thing as "right" in this context … and that things can always be made *better*.

No job is so small or so menial that it can't be done properly, and there's a real nobility that attaches to people who are driven by the need to do the work well.

Pride of workmanship is an aspirational truth.

Visionary Melbourne retailer E.W. Cole [73] said this in the late 1800s:

"Do good and you will be happy and make others happy."

… and I reckon that much the same thing applies to the doing of good **work**.

I find this notion so appealing that I have adapted it for the General Thinking [63] network of thinkers and doers that are gathering online. The lapel pin that accompanies the dispatch of the individually numbered General Thinker keyrings is presented on a letterpress printed card that contains the following **General Thinking Manifesto**:

Do Good Work | Share the Ideas | Help Other People | Make a Difference | Have Some Fun

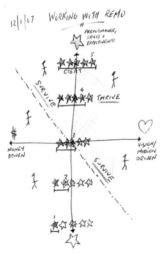

Guidance for REMO collaborators
January 2007

Delivering my welcoming remarks at TEDxSydney 2012

E.W. Cole [73]

The Sun Herald
December 2009

General Thinker keyring
Do Good Work. Have Some Fun.

General Thinking
Manifesto

1 2 3 4 5 6 7 8 9 10 11 12 13 14 15 16 17 18 19 20 21 22 23 24 25 26 27 28 29 30 31 32 33 34 35 36 37 38 39 40 41 42 43 44 45 46 47 48 49 50 51 52 53 54

2012

Photo: Cynthia Sciberras

[69] General Story

Back in 2004 when a more REMO-centric book was going to be called *General Story: A Founder's Tale* I was asked by my then literary agent Fran Moore to put together a short form bio that she could take around to prospective publishers.

This was the RemoGram that I prepared in response to that request.

There's been some water under the bridge since 2004, but you get the idea.

A picture tells a thousand words … and even relatively uneventful lives look more interesting with the help of a little bit of colouring in.

PS: In 1990 I turned 30. On my birthday I sat alone in my Bondi Beach flat and wrote a list of things that I wanted to focus on for the remaining decade of the 20th century. Things worked out on most fronts.

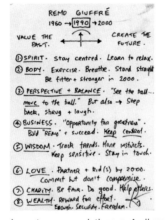

Turning 30 ten year resolutions, 25 April 1990

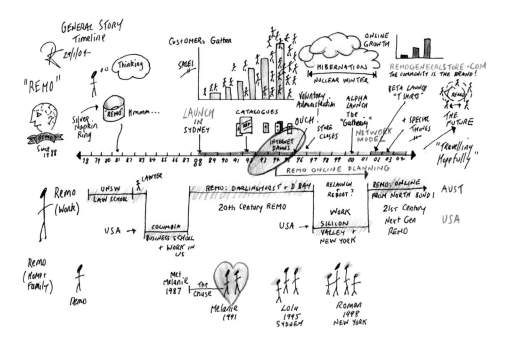

Timeline needs updating!

General Story book dummy, May 2004

1 2 3 4 5 6 7 8 9 10 11 12 13 14 15 16 17 18 19 20 21 22 23 24 25 26 27 28 29 **30** 31 32 33 34 35 36 37 38 39 40 41 42 43 **44** 45 46 47 48 49 50 51 52 53 54

1990   2004

[70] Free Hugs at REMO

Who remembers Free Hugs Guy?

There's a good chance that you already know the story of Sydneysider Juan Mann and the gesture that he turned into a worldwide movement. At the time of writing, the YouTube video that features his original story had been viewed over 75 million times. Juan's free hug gesture has been celebrated and mimicked all over the world. Free Hugs has become a global phenomenon.

So, how did it all start? Here's how Juan explained the genesis of his calling:

"I'd been living in London when my world turned upside down and I'd had to come home. By the time my plane landed back in Sydney, all I had left was a carry on bag full of clothes and a world of troubles. No one to welcome me back, no place to call home. I was a tourist in my hometown. Standing there in the arrivals terminal, watching other passengers meeting their waiting friends and family, with open arms and smiling faces, hugging and laughing together, I wanted someone out there to be waiting for me. To be happy to see me. To smile at me. To hug me. So I got some cardboard and a marker and made a sign. I found the busiest pedestrian intersection in the city and held that sign aloft, with the words "Free Hugs" on both sides. And for 15 minutes, people just stared right through me. The first person who stopped, tapped me on the shoulder and told me how her dog had just died that morning. How that morning had been the one year anniversary of her only daughter dying in a car accident. How what she needed now, when she felt most alone in the world, was a hug. I got down on one knee, we put our arms around each other and when we parted, she was smiling. Everyone has problems and for sure mine haven't compared. But to see someone who was once frowning, smile even for a moment, is worth it every time."

I love this story, and it reminded me very much of Eternity [31]. No surprise then that I had made it my business back in 2007 to track Juan down here in Sydney and offer to develop and promote the sale of a REMO T shirt in tribute to his endeavours.

Also we really liked each other. Juan's no-expectations, Jesus-like demeanour was a good foil for my mercantile approach to his iconic design and its message. And, I'd like to think that, for a while there, the trickle of royalties that we were able to send him made a small contribution to his seemingly monastic existence.

Find the thing. Do it with love. Make people happy ... and you will be happy.

BRC #010, June 2009

FREE HUGS Guy HERE LIVE
Thursday 11 June: 5PM to 7PM
Saturday 13 June: 11AM to 1PM
Free Hugs, Photos, T Shirt Signings, Fun!
.COM/FREEHUGS

REMO Bondi Road Corner Poster, June 2009

| Free Hugs guy | REMO T shirt | Juan Mann | With Juan in 2007 | Juan at REMO in Bondi, 2009 |

1 2 3 4 5 6 7 8 9 10 11 12 13 14 15 16 17 18 19 20 21 22 23 24 25 26 27 28 29 30 31 32 33 34 35 36 37 38 39 40 41 42 43 44 45 46 47 48 49 50 51 52 53 54

2007 2009

[71] Customer Engagement

Customer involvement in the development process at REMO [25] was the plan from the very beginning. In 1989, barely a year after we had been open, I wrote in a catalogue:

"As well as utilising our own internal resources, we plan to draw increasingly upon the resources of our customers in the future, via: newsletters, questionnaires and an in-Store product development feedback booth ... Daily we are reminded that [our customers] know more than we do about what they want in a product."

The launch range for REMO comprised largely of the things that I had personally become passionate about. By 1994 the majority of the things that we were selling owed their existence within our range to a suggestion from a customer other than myself.

When the Internet came along it became much easier for online REMO to engage in this way with the customers of the Global Community General Store [60]. Our own branded offer [30] had been very popular with the customers of 20th-Century REMO, but with the much smaller online business we were not able to bring everything back at once, so we did so in the order that customers voted for. Also, we often had to limit the choices for the relaunched item, and we would engage our customers on that front too. For instance, when the classic REMO Fringed Beach Towel returned it did so bearing trim colours that had been voted up by customers in our online development area. (Royal blue was the firm favourite.)

But surely the most engaging thing we developed for customers, was our 2007 online Design'O'Matic. It was a place on our website (built in Flash by Sydney designer Rob Muller) where customers could create their own T shirt designs using words, shapes and their own uploaded images. Within two months of launch, the customer design category was outselling every other design in the range.

Finally, there's the engagement within the development process of the business itself. Radical transparency was part of our DNA from day one, and there are many examples of that throughout this book. Being completely candid about our operation, and letting our customers see under the hood broke down the traditional wall that normally distances a brand from its customers. For us it was always a case of B being *equal to* C [56].

When you're able to do this, the customers that stay with you are the ones that are taking the journey with you. They stand beside you and become your friends.

REMO CustOMER bumper sticker, October 1996
(Can't believe it took me 8 years to notice that the last four letters of customer was REMO backwards.)

Online REMO Design'O'Matic interface, July 2007

THE JOURNEY

This is the path we'll be taking together. You are an integral part of this PROCESS.

I used this RemoGram to explain to customers why they could only buy our T shirts online to begin with.

[72] The Printed Thing

In 2007 I put a proposal to Hardie Grant Books. Founding director Sandy Grant was a believer in the philosophy of REMO, and had long thought that a book in celebration of that spirit might have some legs. The pitch was this: I would look after content, design and production, and they would take on sales and distribution for some kind of REMO printed thing. "Printed Thing" was a placekeeper name used as a heading for a REMO customer forum that I had set up early the year before as a brainstorming platform for what this, in fact, could be.

I wanted it to do a lot of things. Many of our customers were too young to have experienced our award winning catalogues [43], so I wanted the printed thing to repeat some of that 20th century magic. But I also wanted it to tell some stories and celebrate our history. Finally, I decided that I also wanted it to function as almanac and planner for 2008, sort of a companion to our popular Tempus Fugit wallplanners [36].

As I had done so many times before, I opted for this hybrid approach rather than having to choose. On the back of the Printed Thing (yes, this became its formal name) I wrote:

*"Q: Is it a **planner**? Is it a **catalogue**? Is it a **magazine**? A **year book**? An **almanac**?*
*A: Yes, Yes, Yes & YES. It's the first ever annual REMO **Printed Thing!**"*

But alas, there was no Printed Thing in 2009, nor the year after. This time around the hybrid strategy had failed. This was no set of Splayds [35]. People found the promotional calendar format too confusing. We sold some, but not a lot, and ended up enclosing most of them as promotional gifts in our online orders.

People had also been confused, but happily so, by the hybrid nature of the physical REMO Store. Twenty years earlier, in the 1989 Catalogue I wrote:

"We are different from any other store anywhere in the world … We try to interest and to stimulate without confusing. We don't fall into any category. No retailing formula has been followed & the result is unique. We grow stronger by the week. But what are we actually? – A department store? A museum shop? A gallery? A gift shop? A lifestyle-supply depot? A pharmacy? A newsagency? In truth, we're still working it out ourselves; so don't feel alone in your puzzlement."

You win some. You lose some.

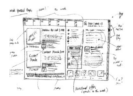

Doodle of Printed Thing
spread, 2007

2008 Printed Thing launch at
Icebergs Dining Room and Bar

GLOBAL COMMUNITY
GENERAL STORE ®

QUALITY & PASSION
SPECIAL THINGS

REMO
Since 1988

PRINTED THING
Some Early Feedback

HGB

★★★★★
"The BEST thing we've ever produced. Unlike anything you've ever seen."
Remo Giuffré
Founder, REMO General Store

★★★★★
"AMAZING ... but we expected nothing less."
Sandy Grant
CEO, Hardie Grant Books

★★★★★
"FABULOUS. Can't wait."
Pat Mackle
Founder, Avant Card

★★★★★
"INSPIRATIONAL. It's not surprising that REMO is now an online store with a large community of inspired customers in all parts of the world."
Kevin Roberts
CEO Worldwide, Saatchi & Saatchi

★★★★★
"FANTASTIC. The ultimate toilet book."
Dare Jennings
Founder, Deus Ex Machina & Mambo

WWW.REMOGENERALSTORE.COM/2008

Promotional Avantcard, November 2007

REMO 2008 Printed Thing endpapers and sample spreads, November 2007

[73] Tribute to E.W. Cole

While doing the research for the REMO *Printed Thing* [72] in 2007 I came across the story of a remarkable man. I was struck by the parallels to my own retail journey, and it made me realise that some of my philosophies, convictions and ambitions were not at all new.

Edward William Cole was born in England in 1832 and died in Victoria in 1918. Entirely self made, he combined philosophy, philanthropy and humour with business acumen – given the outcomes, clearly more than I possess – in the development of a truly unique retailing empire. After virtually monopolising Melbourne's book trade for many years, he is remembered today (but possibly not enough, and hence this tribute) as a visionary yet eccentric public benefactor. At the multi-level glass-roofed Cole's Book Arcade, books were displayed against a background of glittering baubles, live monkeys, stuffed crocodiles, funny mirrors, carnival exhibits and rainbows (a Cole trade mark). Cole turned a "bookshop" into the cultural centre of the City of Melbourne.

Cole's Funny Picture Book (1879), a compilation of words and pictures designed to inform, amuse and inspire, was a breakout success, and was kept continuously in print for almost a century. Many grew up with a great love for these books.

Cole was a gifted merchant and the popularity and mass appeal of Cole's Book Arcade was phenomenal ... all the more remarkable given his adherence to what were then some fairly radical philosophies.

The basic theme of all Cole's philosophy was the desirability of a federated world. Various Cole slogans peppered the retail space. Minted coins (used, by way of crowd control, to gain entry to the arcade itself) also bore snippets of Cole's thinking. Here's a quote from one of the essays that he would personally hawk from the counters of his Book Arcade:

"The possibility and desirability of the Federation of the World will soon become among all nations a confirmed conviction ... The fact is already fast dawning upon mankind, that the natural differences between nations, mentally, morally, and physically, are very little greater than those between brothers of the same family. Nor will the difference of religion prevent the unity of the race ... The morals and leading principles of all religions are in the main strikingly and astonishingly similar, pointing to the inevitable conclusion that they one and all have been evolved from religious instincts existing in the human mind, and further proving that the mind, in its reasoning, its hopes, and aspirations, is essentially alike in all mankind."

E.W. Cole said: *"Do good and you will be happy and make others happy."*

... and I acknowledge that these words have inspired the wording of a motto that I am also promoting in my work with General Thinking [63] i.e. *"Do Good Work. Have Some Fun."*

ADVANCE
KNOWLEDGE,
LET PREJUDICE PERISH,
LET JUSTICE AND CHARITY
ENCIRCLE THE EARTH
AND
EXTEND
TO THE MEN
OF EVERY
CREED,
E.W.COLE, BOOK ARCADE, MELBOURNE 1874

REMO T shirt design, 2007

| E.W. Cole | Cole's Book Arcade Circa 1883 | Cole's Funny Picture Book | Sample Page | REMO T shirt |

1 2 3 4 5 6 7 8 9 10 11 12 13 14 15 16 17 18 19 20 21 22 23 24 25 26 27 28 29 30 31 32 33 34 35 36 37 38 39 40 41 42 43 44 45 46 47 48 49 50 51 52 53 54

2007

[74] Bondi or Bust

In early 2009 REMO online sales had started to soften. We were operating out of a small warehouse on Holt Street in Surry Hills, and so the only sales we were getting were our online sales. Money was tight and there was no more capital. My patient investors, led by Anton Rosenberg at Claymore Capital, agreed that the best survival strategy was to take some kind of decisive action. The decision was made to shift our base to a storefront in Bondi.

In late March 2009 I communicated with our nearly 40,000 mailing list customers, explaining the move in typically forthright fashion:

"This move is not the result of a well-planned strategy. The genesis of the decision had more to do with survival than success. Here's what happened: December was good for REMO (30% up), but January was ordinary (a rare down month). With the economic clouds forming we revisited our budgeted cash flows and stripped growth away from the top line. That made things ugly. On 13 February the Founder bared his soul (sort of) on twitter:

"That night he slept badly ... imagining worst case scenarios. The next morning to Melanie: "Happy Valentine's Day. I'm worried about the business." The next few days were tough. Cost control is not the answer for REMO. We already run very lean. The answer is a higher level of sales ... but how?

"The answer came to Remo on 17 March whilst recovering at home from a minor hernia operation: shift the warehouse to a retail location and pick up some extra revenue from the street via a service counter. Find somewhere close to home in Bondi so as to facilitate the longer "Mom & Pop" hours that would be required to pull it all off. Glimmering hope. Melanie bought in ... and the next day they went scouting for sites. Melanie spotted the FOR LEASE signs on the Bondi Road location, they immediately saw the potential of the corner site, and the rest (as they say) is history. The high level of exposure that the site will deliver is BONUS. So, the response to a big threat has actually yielded an even bigger opportunity."

Travelling Hopefully [1] once again!

We traded from that corner for three years, until we ultimately just ran out of petrol. It was fun while it lasted ... and that corner did indeed become a neighbourhood landmark. Here's a selection of posters from those final three trading years in Bondi.

PS: Melanie's all time favourite Bondi Road Poster was the Sad Dog that we designed to challenge the local graffiti vandals; and you know what ... it worked.

Please don't vandalise our corner posters

REMO Bondi Road Corner #053 | Sad Dog, October 2011

Selection of REMO Bondi Road Corner ("BRC") posters

1 2 3 4 5 6 7 8 9 10 11 12 13 14 15 16 17 18 19 20 21 22 23 24 25 26 27 28 29 30 31 32 33 34 35 36 37 38 39 40 41 42 43 44 45 46 47 48 49 50 51 52 53 54

2009 - 2012

[75] TEDxSydney

TEDxSydney is the biggest thing that I have worked on since REMO General Store [25].

Since 2010 I have been the licensee and primary organiser for TEDxSydney, an annual flagship TEDx event that has become the leading platform and pipeline for the propagation of Australian ideas, creativity, innovation and culture to the rest of the world.

TED approached me with the opportunity in 2009 and, despite experiencing some early reticence [77], I decided to take it on for three reasons: firstly it would serve to reposition me as someone who was more about ideas than he was about T shirts [46] and serve as a platform for that purpose; secondly, it felt like the right thing to do; and thirdly, it sounded like fun. The breadth and depth of my networks (due largely to my REMO profile) would make it easier for me to pull this thing together than it would be for anyone else.

The momentum that TEDxSydney has experienced over the past five years has been quite awesome. TEDxSydney 2014 hosted 2,700 live attendees within the Concert Hall and The Studio of the iconic Sydney Opera House; 7,000 people attended a TEDxSydney satellite event somewhere in the world; 35,000 tuned in to one or another of the four live streams; and thus far there have been 25m views of the videos uploaded from the same day in 2013. Over 75 team members are now involved in the endeavour, and it's the biggest venue-wide event on the Sydney Opera House calendar.

TED celebrated its 10,000th TEDx event in May 2014. The blog post that they compiled and posted to commemorate that milestone referenced TEDxSydney in its introductory paragraph. TEDx is a global phenomenon, and TEDxSydney has become not just the biggest TEDx event in the world; but, more satisfyingly for me and my team, its gold standard from a quality perspective: the jewel in TED's Asia Pacific crown.

The irony of the fact that TEDxSydney (which as a not for profit endeavour can never enrich me personally) has become so big and successful has not eluded me. In contrast, all of the for profit businesses that I've ever started have insisted on staying small, despite my ongoing endeavours to make them big. Not complaining. Just saying.

The payoff is not financial, but is nonetheless considerable. TEDxSydney has given me the opportunity to work with some amazing people and partners, all professionals at the very top of their game. It's taught me much about the power of collaboration, and the momentum that flows so easily from an idea whose time has come.

Montage of images from TEDxSydney 2013 and 2014

Working on my iPad during speaker rehearsals
for TEDxSydney 2013 at the Sydney Opera House

1 2 3 4 5 6 7 8 9 10 11 12 13 14 15 16 17 18 19 20 21 22 23 24 25 26 27 28 29 30 31 32 33 34 35 36 37 38 39 40 41 42 43 44 45 46 47 48 49 50 51 52 53 54

2010 - 2014

[76] Finding EOLO

This is a story of ancestry, persistence … and a happy reunion.

My father built a classic 60' wooden sailboat in the 40s and raced her in and around Sydney during the 40s and 50s. She was named EOLO after the Æolian Islands off the coast of Sicily (Dad's birth place and home up until his migration to Sydney in 1928). The Æolian islands were, in turn, named after *Æolus* the God of the wind.

EOLO was a star in her day, winning many ocean races and placing overall 3rd in the 1947 Sydney to Hobart Yacht Race. Dad loved that boat, and indeed my parents spent their honeymoon on it in Pittwater in 1949. (Mum was fine with that until some of the crew joined to help out with the sailing.)

Although too young to have any of my own memories of EOLO … I was very aware of the pride of place that it took in my family's history. I'd seen all of the photos and old movies. All very *Adventures in Paradise* and romantic. I became smitten. Indeed, we named our daughter Eola (although she is universally known as "Lola"); our son Roman's second name is Eolo; my family company name is EOLO; and I've schlepped the original wooden tiller from EOLO with me from living room to living room all over the world, as a tangible memory of my father who died in 1986.

EOLO was sold by Dad some time in the 60s to "an American." That's all we knew. Often I wondered what had become of her. Every few years I would Google her name … with no results. Then, one day in late 2010 I was at Justin Rosenberg's wedding, and I was telling this story to the guy sitting next to me. He reminded me that it was bad luck to change the name of a vessel, and that therefore EOLO would *eventually* turn up. That night I tried again … and lo and behold, there she was living in San Diego and for sale. I made contact with the current owners Frank and Cindi Valli and we traded some great stories about our shared connection with this magical sail boat. Frank and Cindi have lived on her for over 20 years, raising a family to boot. Frank is actually a shipwright … so she's in fabulous condition.

I got to see for myself early the following year. I was in Long Beach for the TED Conference, and I was once again telling this story to some dear friends over dinner in LA. Their reaction: *"You have go and see her. San Diego is only a three hour drive from here. We'll take you there tomorrow!"*

I spent a great afternoon on EOLO at that marina in San Diego talking and drinking with people who felt like family. All because of a thing. Some things are so meaningful that they transcend their thingness and become much more than the sum of their molecules.

Storytelling is paramount and sometimes we can use things to connect us to what really matters … and that's the people who are associated with those things.

PS: EOLO has her own Facebook page … set up by Frank and Cindi. Search for *Classic Sailboat Eolo.*

Arriving in Hobart, Sydney to Hobart Yacht Race, 1947
Dad at the back in a jacket smoking a pipe

Uncle Mick

Trophy

The crew of EOLO

EOLO

With Frank and Cindi
in San Diego, 2010

Dad standing far right

EOLO by Cedric Emanuel

Uncle Tony [8] far left

EOLO in 2014. For sale!

EOLO, Long Beach CA

Original tiller of EOLO

Dad with
Giulia

EOLO was a winner

15th Nov., 1948.

CRUISING YACHT CLUB OF AUSTRALIA.

Broken Bay Race.

Won by G. A. Giuffre's "Eolo".

1 2 3 4 5 6 7 8 9 10 11 12 13 14 15 16 17 18 19 20 21 22 23 24 25 26 27 28 29 30 31 32 33 34 35 36 37 38 39 40 41 42 43 44 45 46 47 48 49 50 51 52 53 54

2010

[77] More Like a Starfish

In 2009 TED [45] were looking for someone trusted to lead the development of TEDxSydney. I was very much in the TED family, and very firmly their favoured candidate should I be willing step up as the licensee responsible for delivering the event in Sydney. As an aside, I had known Lara Stein, the Founding Director of the TEDx programme, for 20 years, quite independently of my relationship with TED.

Taking TEDxSydney on was going to be no small thing. I was struggling at the time to keep online REMO afloat and moving forward. Working essentially in a voluntary capacity for something that would involve hundreds of hours of my time and much of my energy, and by definition make me no money at all, was the last thing I needed ... or was it?

REMO was at the time a small online business operating out of a storefront in Bondi [23]. It was ticking over and covering its nut ... but just. The experience economy was taking hold, and selling *things* was only going to get harder. I was starting to feel the personal need to diversify. Although I had done other stuff, my positioning as a retail merchant was still quite dominant. This was starting to feel risky. Maybe I wanted to start spending more time on my ideas and less time selling T shirts.

Also, I wasn't far off turning 50 ... and maybe it was time for this old dog to learn some new tricks. I'd never really operated in a comfort zone. Even so, if I was ever going to *really* challenge myself with something, maybe this opportunity was a good candidate.

And so I took on the licence and started to put the idea out there with my network. Momentum built very quickly. I was known and trusted by a lot of people in Sydney, many of whom are professionally at the very top of their game. It became apparent early on that this was going to be a pretty amazing team.

But, there were a lot of moving parts, and by late 2009 I was really starting to feel the heat. My desire to control and oversee every detail was stretching me very thin. There weren't enough hours in the day. I was having a serious crisis of confidence. I became so stressed during a family break at Tilba Tilba on the South Coast that I started to become anxious about my state of mind. I even called my psychiatrist friend Jon Jureidini for an impromptu phone consultation. TEDxSydney had somehow turned from a challenge into a big and scary project. How was I going to pull it off?

Then, early in 2010, I experienced a breakthrough. At TED in Long Beach I met Rod Beckstrom, the co-author of a book called *"The Starfish and the Spider: The Unstoppable Power of Leaderless Organizations."* We got talking. Chop a spider's head off and it dies. Chop off the arm of a starfish, and that arm grows into another starfish.

I read the book and generated this RemoGram on the plane trip home to Sydney.

I had rapidly come to the necessary conclusion that only way to oversee a voluntary event of this scale was going to be by way of trust and **radical** delegation. Literally as soon as the plane landed I started making the calls and writing the emails to the relevant members of the team, giving them all the power they needed to *get this thing done.*

In order to survive, I had to let go.

General Thinker ⨎ remogiuffre.com/starfish

14 Feb '10

R More like a starfish

Starfish RemoGram, 2010

| Feeling the heat at Tilba Tilba | At TED 2010 | Catalyst | Breakthrough | Thanking the team at TEDxSydney 2010 |

1 2 3 4 5 6 7 8 9 10 11 12 13 14 15 16 17 18 19 20 21 22 23 24 25 26 27 28 29 30 31 32 33 34 35 36 37 38 39 40 41 42 43 44 45 46 47 48 49 50 51 52 53 54

2010

[78] Gift Giving Makes You Happy

The central paradox of the REMO General Store [25] was the fact that its *raison d'être* was not to sell stuff per se. Its purpose [48] was to delight and inspire a community gathered around shared values made manifest by the souvenirs of the stories that it was telling [33]. Did you get that?

However, REMO *did* need to sell stuff in order to survive.

Also, for someone whose livelihood depended on these sales, I was (and am still) personally quite disinterested in the consumption of things that I don't need. Buy me wine, buy me chocolate, maybe some little special thing ... but please don't buy me *stuff*.

Moreover, the merchandise that we presented at REMO was rarely something to be found at a trade fair. We would more typically find something *real* i.e. "that one thing" [26] at a hardware store or in a pharmacy. Even so, Melanie and I would sometimes find ourselves walking down aisles full of scented candles, potpourri pillows and novelty homewares. This, coupled with the general vibe of the place (*Were these people really our people?*) would give us both that sinking feeling.

Was this really a good enough use of our precious time and energy? Did we even really want to *be* in this business? Existential shopkeeper ennui.

You see, we didn't sell anything that anyone really *needed*. REMO was not a general store in the traditional sense. No one relied on us for salt, ropes or kerosene lamps.

However, our offer *did* address a constellation of higher order customer needs (hence our wild popularity), and the one that was most closely linked to the generation of revenue was the service whereby we became a one stop source for cool and thoughtful *gifts*. A customer named James said this on the Lovemarks [66] website in 2004:

"To give a gift from REMO is a guaranteed hit, to receive one an absolute delight."

In 2011, to further convince myself that what I was doing was worthwhile, I connected this notion of gift giving to the pursuit of happiness, then (and still now) a western preoccupation.

The new slogan "Gift Giving Makes You Happy" was used in a new design for a REMO campaign in November 2011; and here's what I said on the flip side of a free Avantcard postcard that ended up being distributed throughout Australia:

"There's a warm fuzzy feeling you get when you give someone a gift. It's an ancient ritual that generates some very timely 21st Century benefits. The happiness research is in. When you do something for someone else, your brain produces dopamine and other happy-making hormones. And you can satisfy this pursuit of happiness at REMOGeneralStore. com ... Thoughtful gifts for thoughtful times."

I needed to feel that what I was doing was worthwhile. At the time, this rationalisation was good enough for me.

GIFT GIVING MAKES YOU HAPPY

REMOGENERALSTORE.COM

REMO Bondi Road Corner #056, November 2011

Sinking feeling

Crabbe Hole café

Early doodle

Customer feedback

1 2 3 4 5 6 7 8 9 10 11 12 13 14 15 16 17 18 19 20 21 22 23 24 25 26 27 28 29 30 31 32 33 34 35 36 37 38 39 40 41 42 43 44 45 46 47 48 49 50 51 52 53 54

2011

[79] Thinking Wisdom

The development of General Thinking [63] is my homage to wisdom, and here I'm referring to the old fashioned kind of wisdom rather than the one born of the crowd.

In my experience, the crowd does not always make the "right" decision. Old school wisdom is usually (but not always) born of knowledge and experience, more rarely born of intuition, and requires the exercise of balance and judgement.

Wisdom is:

+ Knowing which of the crowd sourced ideas is actually the right one for the project
+ Knowing the feature to retain and the feature to omit
+ Apple launching an iPad without the pre-existence of any compelling marketplace need
+ Knowing when to add a pinch of this or a pinch of that to your Brand Soup [29]
+ Knowing when it's time to leave the party

All pretty intangible stuff.

Also, and once again in my experience, the right course of action is rarely black or white, but rather a particular shade of grey, and it requires: clarity of vision, strong leadership, good editorial judgement and the ability to strike a fine balance between: leadership v. arrogance, global v. local, designed v. undesigned, flexible v. confusing, honest v. strategic, elite v. egalitarian, systemic v. customised and controlling v. collaborative.

In *my* branded worlds, the involvement of customers in business processes is not a total abrogation of control and/or responsibility from the governing centre to the network. It's not anarchy. It's rather a led democracy, and, if truth be known, it need not be quite as democratic as it appears. People driving the system need to be able to extract the useful from the not-so-useful and recognise that not all customer contribution is created equal.

Even the purest form networks need to be steered by people in control who know where things should be heading … and those people need to be old school wise.

I reckon we need to understand, acknowledge, celebrate and reward subjective *wisdom*, as much as we do *knowledge* or *creativity*; and we need to *structure* our systems and societies for the integration of this wisdom in order to better solve problems and meet challenges for ourselves, our organisations and our communities.

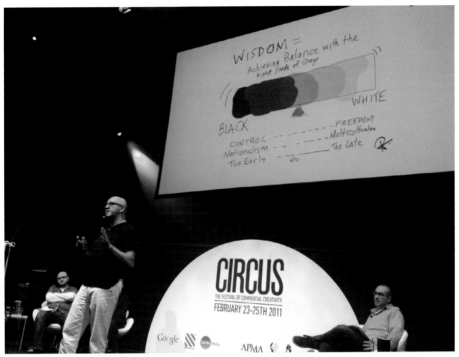

Talking old school wisdom at the Battle of Big Thinking, Carriageworks, February 2011
(My TEDxSydney colleague Julian Morrow sits in judgement on stage.)

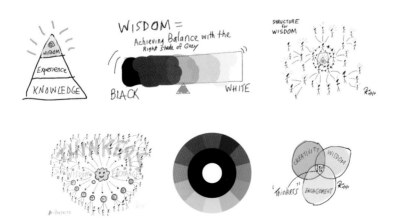

1 2 3 4 5 6 7 8 9 10 11 12 13 14 15 16 17 18 19 20 21 22 23 24 25 26 27 28 29 30 31 32 33 34 35 36 37 38 39 40 41 42 43 44 45 46 47 48 49 50 51 52 53 54

2011

[80] Giuffré Family Bondi Home

The compass is a recurring theme in my life. For all seekers a compass is important.

For my birthday in 1997, when we were going through (yet another) tough period with the REMO business, my genius wife Melanie gave me a small bakelite compass with a note attached suggesting that it might serve to help me *"find [my] way."*

Then in 2001 I had my Travelling Hopefully [1] moment. That was kind of compassy.

And in 2012, when I was working on the network of global cafés [81] idea, I came up with a design for a compass rug design that was inspired by Chris Anderson who had repeatedly claimed that, as the helmsman for TED, he felt less guided by a roadmap, and more by a compass i.e. head in more-or-less the right direction, and the route will be revealed.

For TEDxSydney these days we use a rug bearing the compass design. The tech crew are amused by my need to have it correctly oriented on the stage. Who's that guy on his hands and knees on the rug with his face hovering over that compass on his iPhone?

Finally, to bring it all home (literally) in 2010 I thought that it would be nice to incorporate a compass into the design of our hall runner in Bondi: GIUFFRE FAMILY BONDI ✳ HOME. That compass points due north ... exactly (as if you need to ask); but *only in this precise orientation*. In other words, this rug only "works" in this exact location and in this particular apartment. Everywhere else on earth it would be telling a lie.

For me this was making a statement about the permanence of our move, not just to Sydney, not just to Bondi Beach, but to this apartment in particular. Will we be here forever? Maybe not. Four flights of stairs does not maketh a final resting place *but* I reckon we'll be here for a very long time, and the hall rug is there to celebrate that.

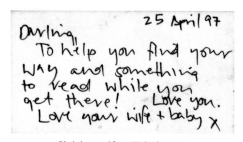

Birthday card from Melanie, 1997

Designer Rugs work order for hall runner

The custom made hall runner at our home in Bondi, July 2014

Compass

To travel hopefully
is a better thing than to arrive,
and the true success is to labour.

ROBERT LOUIS STEVENSON
1850~1894

Travelling Hopefully [1]

TEDxSydney rug

Adjusting

Finding true north

1 2 3 4 5 6 7 8 9 10 11 12 13 14 15 16 17 18 19 20 21 22 23 24 25 26 27 28 29 30 31 32 33 34 35 36 37 38 39 40 41 42 43 44 45 46 47 48 49 50 51 52 53 54

2012

[81] The London Coffee House 2.0

In 2012 I was approached by an organisation who had taken an interest in my work and thinking around cafés, community, technology and culture [85]. They commissioned me to *"develop and articulate a vision, design concept, business model and potential rollout plan for a global network of cafés, potentially incorporating collaborative work spaces and facilities for a global member network,"* agreeing to pay me as the development consultant for virtually all of my time.

What an opportunity! Not my REMO brand [39], but hey, you can't have everything. I seized it with both hands and hit the ground running. Happily, the development of a global and branded network of cafés was something that I'd given a great deal of thought to ... for over 20 years. I spent the next few months putting it all together in collaboration with my networks.

I ran the idea past the City of Sydney, who found the notion of a cultural hub such as this for Sydney so appealing that they offered my client very favourable terms on a four storey building in Darlinghurst (spookily close to the site of the old REMO [25] store). I was able to convince my client that it was going to be a good site for one of these networked café environments. I retained Sydney architect Anthony Gill and noted local chef Jared Ingersoll as a food and beverage partner, and starting looking for the matching local financial commitment required by this client to make the project a reality.

Eventually, in March 2013, and thanks to the efforts of a well connected General Thinker [63], I sourced some funding from a wealthy family in Melbourne. But to no avail. In one of my life's more bitterly ironic moments, during the same Skype call that I broke this GOOD news to my client, they broke the BAD news to me that they had had a strategic change of heart and had decided that they didn't want to proceed with a global rollout of networked cafés after all. Other things had taken a higher priority.

I had suddenly gone from knowing what I was going to be spending 100% of my time on for the next (say) five years (I would have been the Founding Director of the networked cafés initiative) to having absolutely no clue about what I would be doing (and how I would be earning a living) from that moment forward.

I remain philosophical about this experience. After all, people and organisations are allowed to change their minds. However, the experience did serve to remind me why I strongly preferred to be working autonomously on my own ideas.

Lloyd's Coffee House

"During the two centuries (1650-1850) the coffeehouse served Englishmen as a composite office, club and post box ... Unlike the cafés of Continental Europe, the English coffeehouse served business as well as social purposes."

The London Coffee House: A Social Institution, **Deborah Hale**, Rakehell.com, April 2003

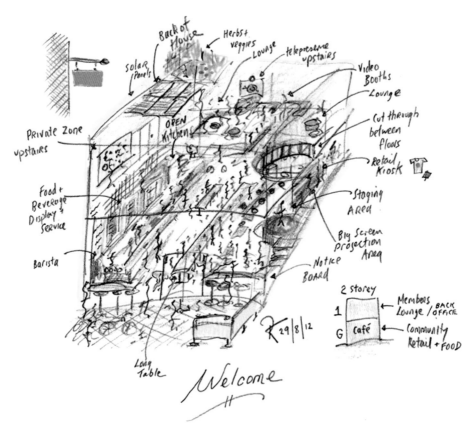

Conceptualisation of networked café, August 2012

Earliest known woodcut image
of a London coffee house

London coffee house, 1660s

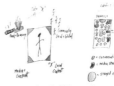

City Café RemoGrams, 2012

Multi city events
via telepresence

Proposal for Sydney

Model of proposed City Café #01 on
Oxford Street in Sydney

Sample schedule

1 2 3 4 5 6 7 8 9 10 11 12 13 14 15 16 17 18 19 20 21 22 23 24 25 26 27 28 29 30 31 32 33 34 35 36 37 38 39 40 41 42 43 44 45 46 47 48 49 50 51 52 53 54

2012

[82] Ask and Ye Shall (Eventually) Receive

You can't imagine how many times and by whom I have been rejected over the years.

Here's a random selection:

In 1980 I asked the comedian Spike Milligan to man the hot dog stand at The Aqua-Ball [12]. He said no ... but oh so graciously. (Wasn't able to locate that letter. Damn.)

I have unsuccessfully tried to raise investment capital for REMO [25] from: countless Australian investors, Country Road Australia (that one actually went to the Board in 1995), Rupert Murdoch (old time's sake?) [19], Barry Diller, Arnold Schwarzenegger (huh?), Luciano Benetton and literally dozens of the VCs in Silicon Valley, New York and Boston.

I asked many US companies to take me on as a consultant brand strategist before I was ultimately employed by the relatively more maverick frog design [53].

My Business School application was rejected by Harvard, but accepted by Stanford and Columbia, and Columbia turned out to be the right fit for me [18].

Finally, and critically, I spent almost four years asking Melanie to be my life partner [38]. She eventually relented. Phew.

The thing is this: You win some. You lose some. *Rejection is actually the norm*. The important thing I reckon is to keep trying.

I guess the thing I've developed over the years is the *stamina* to keep asking for what I want. I've been disappointed many, many times, but I have never been defeated by rejection.

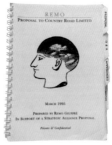

Proposal to Country Road Limited,
March 1995

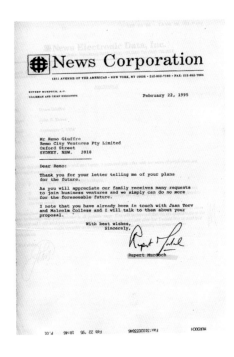

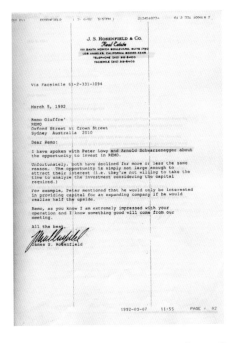

[83] TEDxSydney 2013 Crowd Farmed

In March 2012 Melanie and I received an invitation from Sydneysiders Darryl Nichols and Andrew Valder to *"a community grown dinner ... as part of a little pilot we originated called Grow It Local - a celebration of backyard, balcony, community-garden and windowsill farmers."*

The dinner was happening on a Sunday night at a restaurant called Three Blue Ducks in Bronte, not far from where we live in Bondi.

I was pretty keen to attend, but Melanie needed some convincing. Things weren't looking good for REMO. Our newly relaunched and hyper-socially-integrated website [65] was not doing the numbers it needed to be doing to keep us trading for too much longer. We were starting to feel that we were going to have to put 24 year old REMO to sleep yet again. It was a stressful time, and the last thing Melanie felt like was to be out there putting on a brave face for other people.

But, I managed to talk her into it, and we went along.

It was a great night with such a cool vibe. A totally cosy community love fest. We both felt nurtured and energised by the experience. It added some perspective.

We also met Jess Miller at that dinner. She too was working on the Grow It Local campaign.

Meanwhile, we had decided to move TEDxSydney from Carriageworks to (gulp) the Sydney Opera House, and we were looking to do something special with the food. Uber foodie Jill Dupleix and I go way back, and she agreed to step up to be the Food Curator for TEDxSydney. I introduced her to Darryl and Andrew from Grow it Local, and a bit later we decided to integrate Grow it Local with TEDxSydney 2013, with Jess Miller at the wheel.

This was the genesis for the big crowd farmed lunch at TEDxSydney 2013, a most ambitious and crazy way to feed 2,300 people in 90 minutes. The audience grew much of the food eaten that day on their own balconies. ARIA Catering only knew 48 hours before the event what they were going to be receiving. There were a lot of moving parts, and hundreds of people involved. We even made a short film about it, and that was played for the audience, just before the lunch. Do a video search and you'll find it.

ARIA won best catering at the 2013 Australian Event Awards for the part that they played in this homegrown extravaganza; and people in Sydney still talk about that extraordinary food experience in the most glowing terms.

It *was* pretty awesome ... and quite possibly all due to a chance meeting at a small Sunday dinner in Bronte that we nearly didn't attend. And that's why it's always good to get out amongst the people, even if sometimes it's the last thing you feel like doing.

TEDXSYDNEY CROWD FARMED BY GROW IT LOCAL

GROW IT LOCAL
YOUR LOCAL GROW COMMUNITY

TEDˣ Sydney
x = independently organised TED event

Garage Sale Trail   goody twoshoes   Republic of Everyone

PUT YOUR PATCH ON THE MAP
WWW.GROWITLOCAL.COM.AU

Dinner in Bronte

Jess Miller

Jill Dupleix

Grower Button

TEDxSydney 2013 Food

[84] God is in the Details

One thing that has characterised my work over the years is a consistently obsessive attention to detail [40]; and I have enjoyed working with others who have appreciated (and in some cases shared) that same regard for the small things.

Two cases in point:

1. The layout designer for this book, the camera-shy **Aivi Juske**, has been working freelance as my visual right hand for over 25 years. Although we've worked on a myriad of professional and personal projects over the years, we very rarely meet face to face ... and, in fact, can almost count on one hand the number of our live encounters. Despite this, we work well together, and share a deep appreciation for the importance of the details. This is what generally happens: I send Aivi my doodled RemoGrams, and she works her precise and very particular magic on them. If she tells me something has to be bigger or smaller or different, I generally listen. Respect born of a long history.

2. And for the past 10 years I've been working remotely with a web developer from rural Victoria. His name is **Adam Dennis** and he also appreciates the importance of the details, although I think it sometimes makes him crazy when my obsession with the front end (the shade of grey, the number of pixels, etc.) disturbs his focus on the back end.

And sometimes I encounter collaborators who are *not* used to clients caring so much about the details but who end up having fun with it. The good natured to'ing and fro'ing and repeated production sampling with the guy who makes all of my badges and keyrings has restored his appreciation for the *craft* of his business. For many years he didn't have a client that cared enough to notice, and so he stopped caring himself.

I believe that an attention to detail is required to take something from good to great.

Smell of
the Coffee

Attitude of
the Staff

Sound of
the Music

Look & Feel of
the Space

Tone of
the Advertising

Nature & Quality
of the Product

Feel of the
Shopping Bags

Look & Feel
of the CI &
Graphics

Functionality
of the Website

BRAND

BRAND = PROMISE

COMMUNITY OF CUSTOMERS

Everything Matters: *God is in the Details.*

Mies Van Der Rohe

RemoGram for frog design, 1997

Mies van der Rohe

Adam the Web Guy

Riding the keyring guy hard

1 2 3 4 5 6 7 8 9 10 11 12 13 14 15 16 17 18 19 20 21 22 23 24 25 26 27 28 29 30 31 32 33 34 35 36 37 38 39 40 41 42 43 44 45 46 47 48 49 50 51 52 53 54

1997

[85] Cafés & Community

I have long been fixated by the vision of a global, branded and interconnected network of cafés. It's a recurring theme, and something for me to work on over the longer term.

The idea for a café at 20th-Century REMO [25] was almost as old as the idea for the store itself. We opened it in 1991. It became a place where one could grab a quick coffee, before, during or after a shopping trip at REMO. In those days my inspiration was a cross between the espresso bar at Milan railway station and the United Nations. Communication was a crucial element. We jammed a lot of media into that tiny café: newspapers and magazines from around the world, a television tuned to *CNN*, a daily faxed version of *The New York Times* (how quaint) and a big noticeboard area for posters, leaflets and customer news items. To quote from the November 1991 REMO catalogue [43]: *"In this way the Store becomes more than just a place to buy things; it becomes a cultural exchange point and a communications centre for the community."*

In 1994 I developed this idea as a stand alone small footprint concept. I worked with local operator Mario Venneri and Sydney architect Tina Engelen on the translation of my café RemoGrams (of which there were now many) into the development of what became REMO Mail Order Café #01 on the corner of George and Bridge Streets in the Sydney CBD. I didn't really appreciate it at the time, but it turned out to be Australia's first ever Internet café ... connected via dial up! Apple donated the hardware, and also paid a software developer called Big Animated Digital to help Geoffrey Gifford and me create the first ever version of multimedia "REMO World," thinking that that we would later use it to develop (online) REMO 2.0 [54].

In 2005 I tried once again to get the REMO Cafés thing happening. By now I had a *very clear* idea of how these cafés would operate. I wrote this at the time, in a pitch document for potential investors: *"The elegant integration of the website and the global CustOMER community into the café environment is intended to evoke the feeling that the space is not only a quality local resource and a special place, but also a portal into something much bigger and deeper."* But we had no nibbles, and I put the whole thing on ice.

Then, in 2012 I was commissioned to explore the idea of global network of cafés [81], the inspiration being the London Coffee Houses of the 17th and 18th centuries. Once again, not my brand, but let's do it! I poured myself into the task, and delivered my findings, along with a concrete proposal for a City Café #01 in Sydney; but the project didn't ultimately proceed.

Finally, in 2014, and in connection with my ongoing work with General Thinking [63], I dusted off the plans for the REMO Cafés, but this time with the idea that they could be used as the retail front end for General Thinking club spaces, as with 826 Valencia.

All itches eventually get scratched. Sooner or later I will scratch this one too. Life is a marathon; not a sprint.

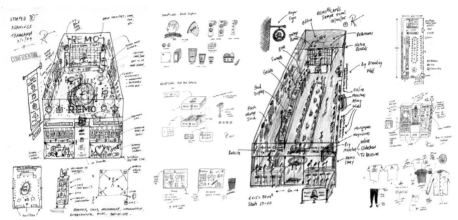

REMO Café RemoGram, 1994

REMO Café RemoGram, 2005

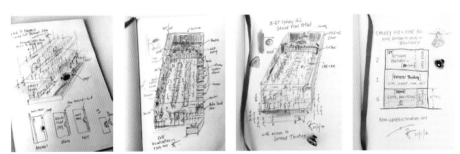

City Café preliminary sketches, 2012

REMO and General Thinking, 2014

REMO Café, 1991

RemoGram
January 1994

Sydney City Café,
concept realised

Australia's first
Internet café, 1994

REMO
Thinking Food

1 2 3 4 5 6 7 8 9 10 11 12 13 14 15 16 17 18 19 20 21 22 23 24 25 26 27 28 29 30 31 32 33 34 35 36 37 38 39 40 41 42 43 44 45 46 47 48 49 50 51 52 53 54

1991   1994   2005   2012 - 2014

[86] The Scorpion and the Frog

The Scorpion and the Frog is a fable about a scorpion asking a frog to carry him across a river. The frog is afraid of being stung during the trip, but the scorpion argues that if it stings the frog, the frog would sink and the scorpion would also drown. The frog agrees and begins to carry the scorpion, but midway across the river the scorpion does indeed sting the frog, dooming them both. When asked why, the scorpion points out that this is its nature.

I've tried on a number of occasions in my life (and usually in response to a dire personal financial situation involving rent, mortgage payments and school fees) to convince head hunters and big company people that my entrepreneurial days are behind me and that I was ready now to buckle down and get a real job. The script goes something like this:

"Yes, it's true that I've run my own things for many years. But, I've got nothing left to prove on that front. It's time to move on. Seriously. What I'd really like to do now is take all of my knowledge, experience and wisdom ... and leverage it within a big organisation and across a large installed base of operations, where just a little bit of Remo magic could potentially generate a whole lot of shareholder value."

And that's when, like the Doctor Edgemar character (Roy Brocksmith) in *Total Recall* trying to convince Schwarzenegger's Quaid that it's all just a dream, I feel a small bead of sweat gathering on my cheek, and I just *know* that the jig is up and that no one is going to be fooled by this converted salaryman routine.

There are good, bad and ugly things about being an entrepreneur. It's a sporadically very rewarding but an often very hard life. Financial security is rarely a feature. Superannuation? What's that?

If you could choose to make it otherwise by making your way to the other side of the river, maybe you would. But generally the fact of the matter is this ... you have no choice.

Remo the scorpion rides another frog

1 2 3 4 5 6 7 8 9 10 11 12 13 14 15 16 17 18 19 20 21 22 23 24 25 26 27 28 29 30 31 32 33 34 35 36 37 38 39 40 41 42 43 44 45 46 47 48 49 50 51 52 53 54

1988 ← → 2014

[87] General Thinker in Uniform

I pretty much wear the same thing every single day, and almost every item of clothing I own is either black or white. Typically I wear white cotton drill trousers and a plain black REMO T shirt. If I throw in a colour, it's a solid, generally bold colour. Never a print.

Other "fascinating" personal details:

+ I only wear black socks
+ I only wear white boxers. They used to be REMO brand. Now they are Brooks Brothers.
+ In these post-REMO days, my white shirts are custom made by J.H. Cutler in Sydney.
+ I wear the same belt every day. It's Il Bisonte leather, like my coin purse and bag.
+ I own maybe 3 pairs of shoes. None of them have laces and all of them are black.
+ For 25 years I've used nothing but Persol frames for my glasses.
+ I haven't worn a tie for 30 years. I regard them as decorative and just a bit ludicrous.
+ I always carry an "Astronaut" Fisher Space Pen clipped somewhere to my shirt.

Are you getting the picture?

I'm a creature of habit, and once I decide that something (or indeed someone) is right for me, I tend to latch on and am reluctant to let go. The reason for change needs to be compelling. I only very recently broke the Persol habit when I came across a frame with a hinge designed by Philippe Starck. It's actually a better mousetrap, so I jumped.

So, what's the deal? Why do I do this?

I actually find it liberating. Not having to think about what I'm going to be wearing every day frees me up to think and obsess about other things that are more important to me.

I reckon you pick your battles, and fashion was not something that I have ever had any interest in. I respect others for whom that is not the case, but for me any attention paid to the twists and turns of the fashion cycle is a waste of creative energy and inspiration.

This is another example where I have developed a system [27] to support the creativity that I would rather be applying to various other aspects of my work and life.

Early 90s uniform

In uniform at the Bondi Icebergs Pool [88] for a photoshoot for *The Australian* (*The Deal* magazine), March 2014

Photo: Nikki Short

| REMO T shirt | White drill pants | Black slip on shoes | Il Bisonte belt | Fisher Space Pen "Astronaut" |

1 2 3 4 5 6 7 8 9 10 11 12 13 14 15 16 17 18 19 20 21 22 23 24 25 26 27 28 29 30 31 32 33 34 35 36 37 38 39 40 41 42 43 44 45 46 47 48 49 50 51 52 53 **34**

2014

[88] Bondi Icebergs & The Sauna Diaries

My favourite place in the world is the Bondi Icebergs, happily very close to where I live.

It's home to Australia's oldest winter swimming club, and the only club that I've ever belonged to that I didn't actually *found*. Every Sunday in winter, a diverse range of members strip to their swimmers and swim a single handicapped race, no matter how cold the water or how wild the weather. It's a salty old school Bondi institution, and I love it. I joined in 1987 with my friend Dare Jennings [21]. (I think that maybe we were being ironic at the time.)

The Bondi Icebergs is also home to a gobsmackingly beautiful 50m seawater pool and a sauna with arguably the best view in the world.

For some years now Melanie and I have started every day by walking our dog Pearl along the promenade (*Piazza del Bondi Beach*) followed by a sauna and a swim at the Icebergs. Melanie has a dunk (or sometimes an "aquachat" in the baby pool with one of her friends) and I do 10 or 20 laps (unless I too just have a dunk, thereby risking being called a "teabag" by the omnipresent rogues gallery of "Bergs" overlooking the pool).

I love that pool. It's a wonderful routine.

You see many of the same people there at the Icebergs in the mornings, and the sauna is the venue for much heated discussion. Every morning there's a different combination of people, so you never really know who or what you're going to get. Some topics are recurrent. Popular topics include: the vaccination debate, the fluoridation of water, other Steve Kilbey conspiracy theories, miracle foods, yoga positions, the merits of pouring water onto the coals (I'm on the "steam team" for this one), politics, music, ethnicity (many represented in there, lots of Eastern Europeans), and so on. It's interesting to see how strangers open up when sitting nearly naked and sweating in a small room with a view to the horizon. And it's a wonderfully social start to the day for someone like me who tends to spend a lot of time working alone.

Recently, we added a feature to the General Thinking [63] website whereby General Thinkers are invited to craft a "Hometown Offer" that is only visible to other General Thinkers. Not surprisingly, this is my Hometown Offer:

"I'll meet you in the morning at the Bondi Icebergs Pool (except on Thursday, which is empty-pool day). We'll have a sauna and a quick swim. I'll introduce you to some of the locals. Then we'll have a coffee and maybe something to eat at the Crabbe Hole cafe overlooking the pool. We'll have a chat and I'll help you come up with a list of some relevant or interesting people to contact, places to see, and things to do during your stay in Sydney."

The Bondi Icebergs is my special place. What's yours?

Bondi Icebergs, Since 1929

Home to pool route.
Three minute walk.

REMO banner, 2011

On the blocks

Steve Kilbey and Yuri the
Russian in the sauna

Melanie, July 2007

Bondi Icebergs Pool

Steve Kilbey again,
sporting GT pin [63]

My special place

Trish Croker and Jill
Dunkerton in REMO Ts

Icebergs at night

1 2 3 4 5 6 7 8 9 10 11 12 13 14 15 16 17 18 19 20 21 22 23 24 25 26 27 28 29 30 31 32 33 34 35 36 37 38 39 40 41 42 43 44 45 46 47 48 49 50 51 52 53 54

1987 ◄—— ——► 1997   2001 ◄——   ——► 2014

[89] Genetics & Passing it On

It's fascinating to see family characteristics being passed down to your kids, although I did shudder a little when my then 13 year old son Roman started marketing a range of "OLAV" T shirts with his mates from school. Maybe one T Shirt Guy [46] in this family is enough.

Like many before me, I have often wondered how much of who we are is due to *nature*, and how much to is due to *nurture*. I guess I'm a believer in both influences. The blueprint of who I would be had been written long before I even existed. However, much of what I have become has been due to influences and experiences that have formed me, many of which are documented in this book of visual memoirs. Remoirs?

And the beat goes on:

Melanie and I are both visual people; and both of our kids have become very competent in that area. Lola was on an art scholarship for all of her high school years, and Roman at 15 years of age is one of the most visually observant people that I've ever known.

Would my children be more (say) into making their own music had Melanie or I been so inclined? Many of our muso friends seem to have spawned muso children.

Roman is also a seawater man, like me and like Melanie's father Joe Dames; but possibly most like *my* father Tom [2], who spent much of his Sicilian youth underwater or on boats in the Mediterranean. Roman is sensitive and empathetic, like his Mum and her Mum, Jessica Dames, but is shrewd like me; whereas Lola has no cunning at all. Lola demonstrates an extreme aptitude for both mathematics *and* art, a bit like me, but more so, and properly. Roman is also wired that way, and is more entrepreneurial.

The inheritance of skill or personality is fascinating, and is one of the really interesting things experienced by people lucky enough and persistent enough [55] to become parents.

Genetics design (from poster)
was a REMO T shirt and postcard

Roman's 8th Birthday card including a
scan of a 1935 Romano's card with art by Dad

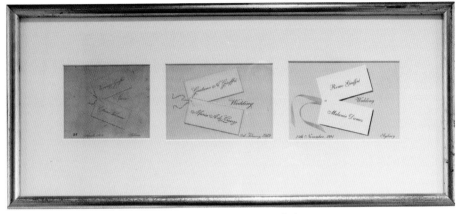

Multi generational wedding invitation design meme
(No pressure Roman)

1906

1949

1991

Dad as a boy
in Salina [2]

Lola self portait,
2004

Roman's bedroom
wall of art in Bondi

Roman the water man
Photo: Sobo Image

Original Genetics
poster at home

1 2 3 4 5 6 7 8 9 10 11 12 13 14 15 16 17 18 19 20 21 22 23 24 25 26 27 28 29 30 31 32 33 34 35 36 37 38 39 40 41 42 43 44 45 46 47 48 49 50 51 52 53 54

2014

[90] Successful Life

I'm really good at some things, but making money is not one of them.

Chronic entrepreneurialism has not been kind to me and Melanie financially, and we continue to be, now well into our 50s, a family that operates on a fairly tenuous month to month footing.

Having said that, we always *just* manage to get by. Something happens, usually at the 11th hour (the sale of something, a consulting gig, a merchandise order, whatever) that enables us to pay the mortgage or those school fees, cover that airfare, avoid that tax penalty, and so on ...

Not that we're complaining one bit. We're both in good health and live a great life ... full of peace, love and abundance; and, to cap it all off, we live at the beach in Bondi [23] for fuck's sake.

We feel grateful and very fortunate about our situation every single day. Blessed in fact.

Does money matter? My sister Giulia sometimes makes reference to an Italian proverb, which translated says: *"Money doesn't make you happy, but it can sure calm the nerves."*

Money is not wealth, and social capital is more valuable than any other sort of capital.

Anyway ... although it is what it is, I do like to hear about people for whom a successful life has little to do with financial comfort or tangible net worth.

Possibly I was feeling especially tuned in to this thinking in late 2009 when I designed this poster for our landmark Bondi Road Corner. I think it hit a chord with a number of people, as I received some really lovely January emails from customers as a result.

This was the NYE email that I sent to all of our customers on 31 December 2009:

"Dear CustOMER, 2009 is soon to be history. It's been a big one here at REMO: getting through the GFC, shifting the business from Surry Hills, and (re)establishing ourselves in Bondi with some born-again REMO bricks'n'mortar. For me personally it has also been an eventful year; one that included a home move (sale & purchase), the taking on of a big new challenge (TEDxSydney 2010) ... and a satisfying amount of weight loss (14kg). 2010 will be tough for REMO (more business challenges ahead); but hopefully very rewarding ... certainly not boring. At this time of year it's good to step back and think about what's really important. We couldn't do better than this quote from Ralph Waldo Emerson, which we have adopted as our Resolution for 2010. Wise and timely. Happy New Year!"

Which brings us to the end of General Thinker. I hope that you've enjoyed reading it, because I really enjoyed writing it; and, if it does OK, you never know ...

As ever, I am full of hope [1].

BRC #029, December 2009

GLOBAL COMMUNITY
GENERAL STORE®

QUALITY & PASSION
SPECIAL THINGS

Since 1988

RESOLUTION

To laugh often and much;
To win the respect of intelligent
people and the affection of children;
To earn the appreciation of honest critics and
endure the betrayal of false friends; To appreciate
beauty, to find the best in others; To leave the
world a bit better, whether by a healthy child,
a garden patch, or a redeemed social condition;
To know even one life has breathed
easier because you have lived.
This is to have succeeded.

RALPH WALDO EMERSON

Wishing Us ALL Happiness & Success in 2010
REMOGENERALSTORE.COM

REMO Bondi Road Corner Poster, December 2009

1 2 3 4 5 6 7 8 9 10 11 12 13 14 15 16 17 18 19 20 21 22 23 24 25 26 27 28 29 30 31 32 33 34 35 36 37 38 39 40 41 42 43 44 45 46 47 48 49 50 51 52 53 54

2009

Index

Index: Continued

Finding EOLO [76]

About the Author

Remo Giuffré is a thinker and creative strategist with a long track record as an entrepreneur, retail merchant and brand builder.

He founded the iconic REMO General Store in 1988; and co-founded the General Thinking network in 2001 (relaunched in 2013). He also enjoys a long and ongoing association with the TED Conferences in New York, and, since 2009, has been Licensee & Director for TEDxSydney, an annual flagship TEDx event (now at the Sydney Opera House) which has become the leading platform and pipeline for the propagation of Australian ideas, innovation and creativity to the rest of the world.

Prior to founding REMO, he worked as a lawyer in Sydney with the global firm Baker & McKenzie and then as a consultant to a number of communications businesses located in both Australia and the US. He was the Director of Branding & Strategy at frog design in Silicon Valley from 1997, and later the resident Brand Strategist at pioneering online developer Organic in New York.

Remo earned combined Commerce and Law degrees from the University of New South Wales, and an MBA with top honours from Columbia University's Graduate School of Business in New York; majoring in marketing, organisational behaviour and communications management.

Although not formally trained as a creative director; he has been dreaming, designing and doodling for much of his life, best exemplified by his "RemoGram" visualisations.

Remo lives in Bondi very near the beach with his wife Melanie, two children: Lola and Roman, and a small black dog named Pearl. He has a sauna and swims every day at the Bondi Icebergs pool.

remogiuffre.com
generalthinking.com/remo

Remo Giuffré

Photo: Tim Lumsdaine